AUSTRIA
1945–1955

AUSTRIA
1945–1955

Studies in
Political and Cultural
Re-emergence

Edited by
ANTHONY BUSHELL

UNIVERSITY OF WALES PRESS
CARDIFF
1996

British Library Cataloguing-in-Publication Data.
A catalogue record for this book is available from the British Library.

ISBN 0-7083-1339-6

Published with the support of the Austrian Institute.

Jacket design by Olwen Fowler, The Beacon Studio, Roch
Typeset at the University of Wales Press
Printed in Great Britain by Dinefwr Press, Llandybïe

Contents

Preface   vii

Note on Contributors   ix

1   Austria's Political and Cultural Re-emergence:
The First Decade
Anthony Bushell   1

2   Narratives in Post-war Austrian Historiography
Robert Knight   11

3   Doderer's Habsburg Myth:
History, the Novel and National Identity
Andrew Barker   37

4   Restoration or Renewal? Csokor,
the Austrian PEN Club and the Re-establishment
of Literary Life in Austria, 1945–1955
Michael Mitchell   55

5   Remembering and Forgetting: Hilde Spiel's
Rückkehr nach Wien in 1946
Andrea Hammel   84

6   *Giraffe unter Palmen:* Saiko's 'Geschichten
vom Mittelmeer'
Stuart Low   99

7   *Eine sagenhafte Figur* (1946) –
An Allegorical Novel of the Status Quo:
The Re-emergence of Albert Paris Gütersloh at
the End of the Second World War
Jörg Thunecke   116

Preface

The coupling of a nation's intellectual and literary life to precise historical dates is rightly regarded as an often desperate attempt to bring order to the ragged edges of human activity. These chronological markers are a convenience. At times they serve as no more than pedagogical aids; in some instances they give the comforting notion of a framework where none may in fact exist. In very few instances do the dates on the calendar and the developments linked to them correspond neatly, yet in the case of post-war Austria there stand behind the dates in the title of this book absolute changes in the nation's position in international law. The collapse of Nazi government in Austria in 1945 and the restitution of sovereign powers in 1955 come as close as any external events can to representing real and discrete stages in a country's cultural as well as political development.

Whilst the story of the immediate post-war years of the two Germanies has been the subject of considerable research activity, the fate of Austria in these years is certainly less well-known in the English-speaking world. It is the intention and the hope of this present volume to throw some light on a period of Austria's history and literature that still deserves to be better known outside Austria. It is also hoped that Austrians might find some illumination in the way the early years of the Second Republic are viewed by those observing from outside her borders.

The editor has great pleasure in recording his thanks to the Austrian Institute in London for its unfailing encouragement and support for this project. He would also like to thank the Director of the University of Wales Press for his readiness to publish this work and Mrs Ceinwen Jones for her considerable editorial assistance.

Anthony Bushell
University of Wales, Bangor – Prifysgol Cymru, Bangor

The Contributors

Anthony Bushell is Professor of German in the School of Modern Languages at the University of Wales, Bangor.

Andrew Barker is Senior Lecturer in the Department of German at the University of Edinburgh.

Andrea Hammel is a Researcher in the German Department of the School of European Studies at the University of Sussex.

Robert Knight is a Lecturer in the Department of European Studies at Loughborough University.

Stuart Low is Lecturer in German in the Department of European Languages at the University of Wales, Aberystwyth.

Michael Mitchell is a Lecturer in the Department of German at the University of Stirling.

Jörg Thunecke is Professor of German at Nottingham Trent University.

Austria's Political and Cultural Re-emergence:
The First Decade

ANTHONY BUSHELL

The re-emergence of the Republic of Austria in 1945 following
the defeat of the Third Reich poses almost intractable problems
for political and literary historians alike. The reconstitution of
Austria within its borders before its incorporation into the German
Reich and its designation as the Second Republic in 1945 suggest
forcibly that those investigating post-war Austria are dealing
with an entity that was and is essentially a continuity of a state
and a community that had existed before the German annexation, the *Anschluß*. Yet 1945 was a new beginning after the
momentous events of the years 1938–45. Understandably, an
Austrian official government publication of 1978, celebrating
sixty years of the Republic of Austria, could with approval quote
Rudolf Neck when he claimed: 'In 1945 Austrians' attitude
towards their country was an entirely fresh one and they faced
their task in an altogether different political spirit.'[1] Simultaneously, the same publication throws up a further problem
when it speaks of the time after 1945 as a period of liberation
(from Nazi Germany) but also as a time of occupation (by the
four victorious Allies: Britain, France, the Soviet Union and the
United States).

This duality – and often multiplicity – of perspective pervades
almost every aspect of Austrian life of this period. The light shed
by a study of Austrian history and literature is largely predeter-
mined by the point from which we choose to start our search
and ask our questions. Very soon along that path of questioning
we discover that there are few neutral, impartial witnesses on
whom we can call. The leading players in the shaping of Austrian

political and cultural life during that decade from the ending of
the *Anschluß* in 1945 to the signing of the State Treaty and the
restoration of Austria's national sovereignty in 1955 had been
shaped by particular events and stages in Austria's pre-war history. Their personal and family fortunes were coloured by the
collapse of the Habsburg Empire in 1918, the political and economic turbulences in the wake of the stringent peace terms set
down in the Treaty of St Germain (1919), the massive territorial
losses of what had been the Austro-Hungarian Empire, the experience of civil strife, the rivalries between the various armed
militia bands and, above all, by the period of authoritarian rule
as politicians such as Chancellors Dollfuß and Schuschnigg
attempted in vain to contain the centrifugal political forces that
were preventing the emergence of a strong and unifying national
identity in the First Republic.

The overwhelmingly negative image offered by Austria in the
inter-war years, despite some areas of progressive social legisla-
tion, provided one set of memories for those men and women
trying to come to terms with Austria in the immediate post-war
era. A second and equally decisive set of recollections would be
of a much more recent vintage; they would be drawn from the
experience of life under National Socialism and the catastrophe
of the war that it had brought with it, whilst for a smaller group
of Austrians there was the experience of exile and, in some cases,
persecution before years spent outside Austria. Several of the
contributions in this book deal directly with these problems and,
in particular, with the legacy of exile for Austrians returning
after 1945 and with the question of what lessons had been learnt
from before 1945 in the new and uncertain days and years following the creation of the Second Republic.

Assumptions regarding many aspects of social and public life
that are taken for granted in lands and cultures which have not
experienced major disruptions to, or dislocations in, their collective life do not hold good for Austria in its immediate post-1945
history. The very idea of an 'Austrian' identity or of an 'Austrian'
literature (as opposed, for example, to literature simply ema-
nating from a territory called Austria) has been cause for endless
speculation – and not a little sophistry – ever since the collapse
of the Empire and the appearance after the First World War of an
unwanted state occupying a small space in central Europe. The

term 'Austria' is itself far from neutral in its connotations; during the Nazi occupation of the country it was eradicated for it suggested an alternative to the concept of a Greater Germany. And its value and function for much of this century has often been negative, to indicate a place that is not Germany, yet unable to state exactly what it is or represents.

Austria's more recent years of political stability, neutrality and prosperity have done much to imbue the idea of 'Austria' with positive connotations to its citizens, but in the immediate aftermath of 1945 the idea of an Austrian nation was far from secure despite the obvious advantages for an occupied country to be able to dissociate itself from identification with Germany. And it is remarkably easy to make mischief with dates and attitudes. Staatskanzler Renner, the man charged in April 1945 with the task of creating a separate Austria, one disentangled from Germany, had, as the first federal chancellor of the First Republic, championed Austria's incorporation into Germany as the only possible course for Austrians to survive the repercussions of defeat in 1918. Taken out of context this apparent volte-face in such profound matters as national allegiance verges on the farcical, suggesting by turn flagrant opportunism or profound cynicism. Only when the twists and turns of Austria's fortunes in this century are fully appreciated do we come to see a nation with very little room for manœuvre, more often than not placed in a position of having to react rather than initiating in almost all the major aspects of its political and social life. External factors often deprived the key actors in Austria's history in this century of the luxury of a consistent position. The extreme expression of Austria's plight can be found in the attempt in the 1930s to seek protection from Mussolini's fascist Italy as the best way of preserving Austria from German incursion, an attempt which compelled Austria to put aside the indignation she felt at the territorial loss of South Tyrol to Italy following the First World War.

Once Austria had been freed of National Socialist control there was no consensus as to which Austria was to be restored: the Austria existing immediately before the German invasion, that clerical and conservative *Ständestaat* in which communists and socialists had been driven underground, or the earlier Austria that had first emerged out of the collapse of the Habsburg Empire? The decade of occupation by the Allies, in striking contrast to the four years that saw Germany transformed from four zones of occupation to the two independent states of the Federal Republic of Germany and the German Democratic Republic, gave a provisional quality to much of Austria's political and cultural activity; it also took out of the hands of Austrians much of the incentive to undertake the difficult and painful task of self-scrutiny whilst the fate of the nation as a whole still rested in the hands of its occupiers.

Not only was Austria's period of occupation longer, it also followed a very different course from that of Germany in the immediate post-war period. The isolation of Berlin from the rest of the Federal Republic led to the revitalization of cultural life in West Germany; cities such as Munich and Hamburg were happy to absorb much of the artistic energy of the former capital, whilst the eclipse of former centres of artistic and publishing life such as Dresden and Leipzig gave room for new centres to establish themselves in the West. The location of a provisional capital in Bonn saw the emergence of a flourishing political and financial world in the Rhineland. The literary, economic and political landscape of the new Germany after 1945 was thus radically different in appearance from that of pre-war Germany. These new arrangements resulted in a new voice emerging from Germany, one no longer centred on Prussia and, following massive movements and expulsions in population, with a far stronger Catholic presence (to be heard confidently in the very decentralist tones of a journal such as the *Frankfurter Hefte*). Germany's intellectual and physical proximity to France has been viewed with some justification as the most distinctive influence on Western Europe's post-war history.

When a sovereign Austria was finally proclaimed in 1955, as the last of the occupying troops left its territory, no changes of comparable magnitude had taken place. The Austrian zones of occupation had not been formalized into separate and sovereign entities as in the case of the two Germanies. And despite initial misgivings, especially on the part of the Americans, that Renner and his provisional government emerging in the Soviet-occupied territory could not be trusted and that alternative centres such as Salzburg should be promoted to rival 'red' Vienna, the traditional position and power of Vienna in political and literary life was restored. The major transitions in Austria's economic life, including the investment in heavy industry, had taken place before the Allied invasion of the country; it had been during the Nazi occupation of Austria that the gearing of the Austrian economy to the German war effort had occurred, bringing with it investment in the country's infrastructure. Furthermore, the status of Austria as a predominantly Catholic-minded society was not seriously challenged in the post-war era. In one important respect, however, the post-war Second Republic was quite unlike the pre-war First Republic: Austria's Jewish community and its intelligentsia had been decimated.

Two problems faced the creation of an Austrian identity and the setting of a clear cultural agenda in the immediate post-war period. The First Republic had been too short-lived to provide a comprehensive and unshakeable foundation for the politically and culturally active in 1945. (And as many of the themes in post-1945 literature suggest, Austrians were still struggling to come to terms with the upheavals of 1918.) Evocations of an earlier Austria à la 'es ist ein gutes Land'[2] ran the risk of posthumously rehabilitating the Habsburg Empire and thus calling into question the moral legitimacy of a republican Austria. Few of the institutions had survived the inter-war years untarnished: the universities had been a fruitful breeding-ground for National Socialism, the police and judicial system never commanded respect amongst much of the socialist-voting population after the Schattendorf verdicts, when right-wing militia men were acquitted of murder after shooting on a socialist demonstration. Many writers and artists had simply declared themselves to be supporters of Hitler and threw in their lot with the National Socialists. Nor could Austria point to a figure of the international stature of a Thomas Mann who could be said to have represented the integrity of a better Germany in exile. One of the striking features of Austrian literary life in the early years after 1945 was its reluctance to promote the best of its writers who had spent the war years in exile. The University of Vienna, for instance, rejected an appeal in the late 1940s to award an honorary doctorate to Hermann Broch. And in general there was little enthusiasm to welcome back those who had fled the Nazis and had spent the war years in exile. Those who had remained in Austria tended to ignore the dislocations and hardships of exile, which had driven some prominent names to suicide. Nor

was there enthusiasm to relinquish power to those who had
been in exile. To quote one leading historian: 'Als die Exilgrößen
wieder in Österreich auftauchten, hatten die Österreicher selbst
ihr Haus schon bestellt; die Kommandoposten waren vergeben.'[3]

The Allies' denazification policy represented a second problem, for it disenfranchised very large numbers of the Austrian
population. The three political parties emerging after 1945, the
conservative People's Party, the Socialists and the Communists,
were quick to realize that this inevitably antagonized and
aggrieved sector of the nation, including many of their depend-
ants, would constitute a significant element in a future elec-
torate. This political calculation helped to weaken any resolve on
the part of any one of the parties to be seen as the persecutor of
those labelled as compromised by their former work in the Third
Reich.

If the room for manœuvre in the political sphere was cur-
tailed, a greater weight was naturally placed on culture to bring
about certain desired changes in the nation's attitudes. Culture,
especially the written word, and the educational sector as a whole
were to be enlisted in a conscious effort to foster and promote an
idea of Austrian nationhood. Thus, as early as June 1945, the
conservative Austrian People's Party could proclaim in the eighth
of its fifteen guiding principles the 'zielbewußte Pflege des österreichischen Geistes und schärfste Betonung des eigenständigen
österreichischen Kulturgutes, das in dem als Vätererbe auf uns
überkommenen christlich-abendländischen Ideengut begründet
ist'.[4] By placing such expectations upon artists and writers, the
political parties after 1945 were repeating, no doubt unwittingly,
the practice of the National Socialists: art was expected not to
fulfil primarily its own criteria but to play its part in the forming
of the national consciousness. It is not surprising, therefore, that
in the first decade of the Second Republic writers of often minor
talent found preference over greater writers if their work demon-
strated a pronounced Austrian patriotism. Sigurd Paul Scheichl
is quite right in claiming that the Austrian state at this time gave
far greater regard to patriotism than either to the concept of
democracy or to anti-fascism in its effort to create an Austrian
identity.[5] Scheichl is also correct in drawing attention to the number of leading figures and influential functionaries in the state
apparatus, and in particular in the ministry for education, who

had held post during the time of the *Ständestaat* and now held offices or posts in the early post-war governments.[6] Few radical departures could be expected from those who, admittedly no friends of the Nazis, had been at home in the clerical and authoritarian Austria of Dollfuß. By their nature these men and – to a much lesser extent for few reached senior office – these women were conservative in outlook; their main interest was the restoration of an older Austria. Yet to gain favour with the Allied control powers it was often sufficient to demonstrate a vigorous pro-Austrian attitude, which by definition meant anti-German, and, unlike the situation after 1918, there was little difficulty in finding Austrians prepared to denounce the miseries that life in a Greater Germany had brought.

A bias towards a notion of 'restoration' was far from being the exclusive concern of the right of Austrian politics. Even the most influential of the Austrian communists, Ernst Fischer, education minister in Renner's first and short-lived government of 1945, understood that it was only through an evocation of an 'Austrian tradition' that a work-force infected by years of Nazi propaganda could be rehabilitated politically. In this respect he found himself making common cause with Catholic intellectuals in Austria. 'Restoration' was also to be understood literally: the enormous amount of money and energy devoted to the rebuilding of the Stephansdom and the Burgtheater in Vienna, despite the catastrophic housing shortage, gives a clear indication of the aspirations of many Austrians, for it was in the rebuilding of these symbols of an older Austria, rather than in clearing the ground for a new Austria, that the imagination of the nation resided. A tone of disdain towards attempts to create a new nation, especially when this meant calling on the theatrical props of an older Austria, can be clearly heard in the words of the conservative writer Fritz Habeck, whose family chronicle novel *Der Ritt auf dem Tiger* betrays an indifference towards the new Austrian republic which was felt in many circles:

> Unmittelbar nach dem Einmarsch der Russen kümmerte sich niemand um die Ernährung der Millionenstadt . . . Nach einiger Zeit meldete sich die eigene Regierung, und eine ihrer ersten Amtshandlungen bestand darin, die Briefkasten wieder gelb zu streichen, die im Jahre 1938 von den deutschen rot bemalt worden waren.[7]

The hardships of the years after 1918 and the uncertainties brought about by what appeared to be a never-ending occupation after 1945 may explain in part the weariness and circumspection of many citizens. Their joys and frustrations in that first post-war decade are now almost forgotten to the outside world, in particular the anxious wait for those Austrians who had served in the *Reichswehr* and had been made prisoners of war by the Soviets. Some did not return until ten years after the end of the war; others were never accounted for. The successes of Austrian sporting heroes, especially in winter sports, meant a great deal in the early years of the Second Republic, whilst participation in international sporting events gave the republic and its citizens a sense of pride in the reborn nation.

The re-establishment and celebration of a sovereign Austrian state was certainly not always reflected in the work of writers, and most notoriously so in one of Austria's most prominent post-war authors, for Peter Handke had noted in his *Persönliche Bemerkungen zum Jubiläum der Republik*:

> Der Staatsvertrag wurde von unsereinem eher als sportliches Ereignis aufgenommen, das man neugierig verfolgt, solange es im Fernsehen übertragen wird. Aber wenn man abschaltet, ist man in seiner eigenen Welt wieder ganz verriegelt. Diese eigene Welt war ein Österreich, in dem man sich auch ohne Russen und Engländer besetzt fühlte, von den Besatzungsmächten der materiellen Not, der Herzenskälte der Religion, der Gewalttätigkeit von Traditionen, der brutalen Gespreiztheit der Obrigkeit, die mir nirgends fetter und stumpfsinniger erschien als in Österreich.[8]

This picture of a cold, uncaring, early post-war Austria is by no means restricted to the *enfants terribles* amongst the country's best-known writers, although the works of both Handke and Thomas Bernhard have been merciless in their criticism of the country. Images from other writers show an early post-war Austria that has not developed beyond a feudal society in which a crypto-serfdom is practised (as in Franz Innerhofer's novel *Schöne Tage*) or where the very soil revolts against the war crimes that have been committed upon it (Hans Lebert's *Die Wolfshaut*). These works were published after the 1950s, and Handke's generation in particular were part of a revolt against the established writers of the young Second Republic. The revolt was partly political, partly artistic in nature, but its distorting effect upon the reception of Austrian literature in its first post-war decade has been immense, for later generations of readers have come to the works of the immediate post-war writers via the filter of rejection of those authors whose age had left them uncompromised by the National Socialist years.

The younger writers also recalled how the political and literary institutions had done little to promote the avant-garde in Austria. The seeming institutionalization of Grand Coalition government in post-war Austrian politics discouraged too frank an examination of Austria's recent past for fear of upsetting the boat. Younger talents had experienced the frustration of critical hostility and public indifference to experimentation in the arts. Yet although the early post-war years had not been without champions and advocates for new literary forms well established in other countries – in this context the many short-lived journals come to mind, victims, as in the case of many experimental journals in West Germany, of currency reform – the same need for a period of restoration in public life was felt keenly too in the arts. In rejecting the political attitudes of the early Second Republic, writers coming to maturity after the signing of the State Treaty rejected the preferred literary models of that period. Thus Austrian literature, digesting with varying degrees of comprehension Wittgensteinian ideas concerning the reliability of language, began to doubt narrative and the coherent relating of experience which turns history into stories and allows stories to illuminate history. This reluctance to make the link between *Geschichte* as history and *Geschichte* as story-telling is palpable in Michael Scharang's uneasy preface to his edition *Geschichten aus der Geschichte Österreichs 1945–1983*: 'Entsprechend der Kompliziertheit der österreichischen Geschichte hatte die Literatur immer ein recht vertracktes Verhältnis zur Historie. Werke, aus denen sich die historischen Vorgänge direkt ablesen lassen, bilden die Ausnahme.'[9]

The implications of the rejection of narrative was the more or less wholesale dismissal of the literary output of the majority of Austrian writers in the 1950s by the rising generation of writers of the 1960s and 1970s. Unfortunately, this rejection fell into the trap of encouraging an across-the-board dismissal of the period as a whole. It is the hope and intention of this book that polemic and exaggeration, which are the legitimate tools of creative writers,[10] will be placed to one side as some of the most interesting voices active in these formative years of the Second Republic are the subject here of fresh examination.

Notes

1 *Sixty Years of Austria* (Vienna, 1978), p. 32.
2 Franz Grillparzer, *König Ottokars Glück und Ende*, Act III, line 1671.
3 Helmut Andics, *Österreich 1804–1974*, vol. IV (Munich, 1984), p. 79.
4 Klaus Berchtold, *Österreichische Parteiprogramme 1868–1966* (Munich, 1967), p. 377.
5 Sigurd Paul Scheichl, '"Zu wenig *Österreichverbunden*": Bemerkungen zu kulturpolitischen Positionen im Österreich der Nachkriegszeit', in *Studi Tedeschi*, XXXIII, no. 1–2 (1990), 1–19 (p. 18).
6 Ibid., p. 8.
7 Fritz Habek, *Der Ritt auf dem Tiger* (Vienna, 1958), p. 549.
8 In Peter Handke, *Das Ende des Flanierens* (Frankfurt am Main, 1980).
9 Published in Darmstadt in 1984, p. 7.
10 See especially in this context the comments of Wendelin Schmidt-Dengler in his essay 'Windstille? Zur österreichischen Literatur der Gegenwart', in *1945–1995 Entwicklungslinien der Zweiten Republik*, edited by Johann Burger and Elisabeth Morawek (Vienna, 1995), pp. 119–31 (p. 130).

2

Narratives in Post-war Austrian Historiography

ROBERT KNIGHT

I

Historical writing on Austria's post-war decade has been dominated by four narratives – three of them broadly benign, one of them highly critical. The benign ones are the educational experience (*Lernprozess*), the odyssey through the troubled waters of the occupation, and the journey to sovereignty and neutrality. The critical narrative, a recent arrival, is of a journey which in failing to confront National Socialism took a wrong turning. These narratives are often combined and rarely made explicit. The following attempt to abstract them from a range of writing (without claiming exhaustiveness), to draw out some of their implications and to address some of their weaknesses therefore runs the risk of terrible simplification.

II

The narrative of a collective educative process runs through many accounts of modern Austrian history. While some trace it back to the nineteenth century, to the epic struggle between Prussia and Vienna for the leadership of 'Greater Germany' and a gradual realization of an Austrian national identity,[1] most see National Socialist rule as the crucial lesson. This was a central assumption of post-war Austrian diplomacy, particularly during the first phase of the Austrian Treaty negotiations (1947–9) when Austrian politicians, diplomats and journalists argued that, even if the *Anschluß* had been widely welcomed in March 1938 (which was partly disputed), bitter disappointment had swiftly followed and after disappointment came active resistance. Since Austria had learnt her lesson the occupation should be terminated.

This account was closely tied to the 'Moscow Declaration' of October 1943 (actually the third of four Moscow Declarations) in which the foreign ministers of the Soviet Union, Great Britain and America described Austria as 'the first victim of Hitlerite aggression', and declared their intention to restore it as an independent state. Its final paragraph, however, reminded Austria of the 'responsibility which she cannot evade for participation in the war on the side of Hitlerite Germany, and that in the final settlement account will inevitably be taken of her own contribution to her liberation'. The historical purpose of the declaration, as Robert Keyserlingk has shown, was primarily to stir up Austrian resistance. In this it largely failed. Despite the heroic efforts of some brave groups and individuals,[2] National Socialism remained more or less intact almost up to the end.[3] Western observers concluded that 'unlike the Czechs or Poles, the Austrians have no passionate or positive national feelings'.[4]

After the war, as well as claiming the status of collective victim, Austria's officials sought to show that the last paragraph had been 'fulfilled' in the last eighteen months of the war, rather as if it had been posed as an examination question on Austrian democratic maturity. The historical accuracy of the evidence used to support this view was shaky[5] but in a sense this did not much matter – at least in the short term. There had been no agreed pass-mark by the Allies and post-war assessments were more a matter of *Realpolitik* than historical evidence. In the course of the Cold War the West swung round to the Austrians' estimation of their legal status as victims and (with some reservation) to their account of resistance.[6]

In the long run, however, a tension was created within Austrian society between the claim of the educational narrative that the restored Second Republic reflected the ideals and achievements of the Resistance and the reality of a society in which resistance had been at best marginal. The tension was evident as the foundation stones of the state were laid by a generation of younger pre-war politicians. To these 'founding fathers', Resistance fighters appeared to be either naïve amateurs to be ignored, or a threat because they had a source of legitimacy which bypassed the party politicians.[7] In the early months the danger appeared to come in the form of western secessionism led by the provisional governor (*Landeshauptmann*) of Tirol, Karl Gruber, who had placed himself at the head of the Tyrolean Resistance movement in April 1945. In Renner's eyes, however, it was time to explain to newcomers who had not joined any political party that the Resistance movement had done its work, that it was now a question of reconstruction not resistance, and that the three parties catered for every form of belief. The members of the Resistance movement were recommended to enter one of the three parties:

> Es wird, glaube ich, auch Zeit sein, daß man den Eingängern, die sich keiner politischen Partei angeschlossen haben, erklärt, die Widerstandsbewegung habe ihre Arbeit getan, jetzt heißt es nicht Widerstand, sondern Wiederaufbau, die drei Parteien bietet für jede Art der Gesinnung Raum. Den Mitgliedern der Widerstandsbewegung und der anderen Bewegungen wird empfohlen, in eine der drei Parteien einzutreten.[8]

Gruber himself was successfully 'integrated' and became Austria's foreign secretary from 1945 to 1953. But a few months later the problem presented itself in a new form when some of the Resistance and 'freedom fighters' became infiltrated by Nazis seeking to cover their tracks. The education minister pointed out that it was difficult simply to dissolve the Resistance organizations since 'wir sind doch auf dem Standpunkt daß wir etwas gemacht haben gegen die Nazi ('after all we have taken the position that we've done something against the Nazis').[9] During the Cold War many Resistance fighters and former victims of National Socialism were integrated into the two main parties – which meant an honoured but marginal role, certainly compared with war veterans. Of those who refused to be integrated some joined the communist Resistance organizations and became a thorn in the side of post-war governments, all the more galling because they had foreign contacts and could not simply be dissolved. It was only in the course of the 1960s, as the Cold War subsided, that they too became integrated, in a slightly ambivalent way, partly representing the 'good Austria', partly criticizing widespread social attitudes to the Resistance, for example in strongly 'German national' areas like Carinthia. This ambivalence helps to explain the gulf between the self-image of the early researchers into resistance, who saw themselves as battling against neglect of their subject,[10] and the perception from abroad that the researchers themselves were in some way defending 'official Austria'.[11]

This ambivalence can also be seen in the work of those Jewish refugees who had continued their attachment to Austria after the *Anschluß*. Austrian exile groups in Britain and America (many of them communist) stressed both during exile and afterwards the anti-Nazi attitude of the population and the activities of the Austrian Resistance.[12] They portrayed the Resistance (and Austrians in exile) as in some sense the 'real' Austria, the carriers of the Austrian national idea. Yet they also saw that in post-war Austrian society the Resistance played a marginal role.[13] One way of overcoming the problem was to shift the educational process from a historical event, which was supposed to have happened during the war, to the post-war period where it became a kind of ongoing anti-fascist challenge for the future. The anachronistic proposal to define the actions of Austrian exiles who had been driven out of Austria and fought in Allied armies as part of the contribution asked for in the Moscow Declaration demonstrates the difficulty of this position.[14]

Recent research has undermined the notion of any united collective Austrian reaction to National Socialist rule, whether of support or of opposition.[15] It suggests that much of the evidence of the classical accounts of the educational process is anecdotal or uncorroborated. One example is the much-repeated account by the post-war socialist leader, Adolf Schärf, of his Damascene revelation of Austria's true national identity. On being approached early in 1943 by the German social democrat Wilhelm Leuschner to support the German Resistance, Schärf records, he suddenly realized that 'der Anschluß ist tot . . . die Liebe zum deutschen Reich ist den Österreichern ausgetrieben worden'('the *Anschluß* is dead . . . the Austrians have had their love for the German Reich driven out of them').[16] Other accounts of sudden conversion appear no less implausible.[17] A more convincing, if less dramatic, picture of Viennese life and attitudes in the closing months of the regime is conveyed by Josef Schöner's fascinating diary. This suggests that, apart from the core of fanatical Nazis, grumbling, anti-Prussian sentiment, war-weariness and hatred of party officials were rife. But the dominant mood was resignation, mixed with hope for the end of the war.[18]

In addition the material and ideological bonds between Austrian society and the regime cannot be ignored. German carpet-baggers were not as dominant as once assumed[19] and there were Austrian gainers from the 'arianization' of Jewish property and from the war economy.[20] Many who were not Nazis supported the removal of Austria's Jews, even if they did not necessarily know that all who failed to flee would be killed. According to Evan Bukey there was 'general approval and acclamation of the regime's anti-semitic barbarities, a strong consensus for ridding the metropolis of Jews in a legal and orderly manner'.[21] Discontent did not prevent the regime from functioning almost till the last. Admittedly resistance in the Second World War was a minority occupation in all countries, but the lack of a strong national motivation made this particularly true in the Austrian case.

Finally, perhaps it would be useful to disentangle three distinct elements of education; democracy, Austrian nationhood and collaboration (between socialists and clerical-conservatives). The tendency to conflate them is evident when the disillusionment of Austrian Nazis at their failure to reap the hoped-for rewards of illegal activity (between 1933 and 1938) is seen as evidence of a changed attitude towards democracy.[22] In all three cases the thrust of recent research has been to place the decisive process after the war. Austrian national identity appears to have solidified in the twenty years after the State Treaty; institutions of social partnership only became accepted in the late 1950s or 1960s.[23] If the theory of an educational process retains some plausibility it is perhaps in its third element – collaboration between Austria's élites. But even here the crucial change was hardly the 'Geist der Lagerstrasse' – the proverbial new spirit created after leaders of clerical conservatives (Blacks) and socialists (Reds) had jointly suffered in Nazi concentration camps. It appears more like a common-sense realization that the circumstances of 1945 offered a chance only if civil war and violent confrontation were avoided. Collaboration was not an agreement to 'bury the hatchet', as post-war socialist speeches recalling the suffering of the workers under Dollfuß and Schuschnigg make clear, but a cautious and provisional agreement which had to be developed and confirmed by post-war political practice.[24]

Seeing Austria's educational process as part of post-war history, rather than as a rejection of National Socialist rule has far-reaching consequences.[25] The educational narrative offered an account of an Austrian national experience which claimed to be based not on pragmatism but on historical truth. For that reason a 'realist' defence of the 'victim thesis' based on pragmatic necessity[26] misses the point. A state's legitimation requires more than the defensive argument that 'there was no alternative'.[27]

III

In many narratives Austria's post-war decade appears as an odyssey, a journey through wind and storm, past rocks and sirens, before arrival at a safe haven in 1955. The journey ends with the breakneck series of events which started with the speech of the Soviet foreign minister, Molotov, early in February 1955, the visit of an Austrian delegation to Moscow in April, the signature of the treaty a month later, and the final withdrawal of the last Allied soldier in October.[28] On closer inspection three versions of this narrative can be distinguished: the first is essentially the story of Austria's escape from communism; the second an escape from American attempts to push her into the western camp; the third, more consensual, account is of an escape from the occupation itself and the tutelage of the four occupation powers.

The narrative of Austria's escape from communism became established after 1955. Much of it derives from the fact that the Soviet withdrawal seemed to contradict what had become an axiom of containment – that the Soviet Union never willingly withdrew from any territory it had once seized. That axiom seemed to be confirmed for the Austrian case between 1950 and 1954 when the Soviet government blocked any progress over an Austrian treaty. But this veiled the fact that in the first phase of negotiations (between 1947 and 1949) the Soviet Union had, even in the view of many Western negotiators, been ready to evacuate the country. Furthermore, the delay after 1949 was presumably not because of any objection in principle but due to the Soviet desire to retain a bargaining counter in their attempt to prevent the inclusion of West Germany into the European Defence Community. In 1950, for example, the Soviet ambassador in London assured Austria's foreign minister, Karl Gruber, that 'Wenn es darauf ankommt, so machen wir den Staatsvertrag mit Österreich in zwei Stunden!' ('When the time is ripe, we'll make the State Treaty with Austria in two hours!').[29] In this light the sudden Soviet shift in 1955 does not seem quite so surprising. As for explanations for the Soviet withdrawal, there is almost a surplus on offer; the most plausible two are firstly, the evident propaganda advantage gained for Khruschev's new foreign policy of supporting non-aligned and neutral countries, and, secondly, the strategic advantage of driving a wedge between the NATO partners, West Germany and Italy.[30]

The story of Austria's escape from communism is often extended beyond the diplomatic sphere to suggest a series of narrow escapes from a Soviet and Communist party attempt to take over Austria. The attempts, it is suggested, were thwarted by a combination of luck, skill or steadfastness on the part of Austria's leaders and people. The establishment of the Austrian provisional government in April 1945 under Karl Renner is usually taken as the first major example. Intended to be a pliant figure-head, Renner was supposed to have 'outwitted' the Russians. Subsequent escapes included the Second Control Agreement of June 1946, in which the Soviet authorities apparently blundered into conceding more sovereignty to the Austrians than they had intended, and the failure of a communist *putsch* attempt in October 1950. Two years after the State Treaty, Gordon Brook-Shepherd concluded that the Austrian 'record here is one of constancy and steadfastness which seeks its equal even in this age of moral blackmail and the rubber truncheon'.[31]

In retrospect, and in the light of subsequent research, this view makes assumptions about Soviet intentions which appear questionable. For example there is little evidence that the Red Army ever tried to make Renner a puppet, and even positive evidence that it did not.[32] The events of 1950, it is now widely accepted, may have been partly an attempt to destabilize the government but hardly a *putsch* attempt.[33] Of course Soviet obstructiveness and disregard for Austrian interests is clear, as in the dismantling of industrial plant in eastern Austria. So are the acts of inhumanity and illegality such as the thousands of rapes committed by Red Army soldiers on their arrival in Vienna or the many kidnappings instigated in occupied Vienna by the NKVD. But seeing this as part of a Soviet attempt to absorb Austria was probably an exaggerated attempt to fit the Austrian case into the geo-strategic assumptions of 'containment'. A central example is the Soviet claim to German external assets in their zone, a claim which was legitimized as part of the German reparations settlement at the Potsdam Conference. In the course of 1946–7 the Soviets asserted a maximalist interpretation of the claim, including 260 factories, extensive oil assets and the Danube Shipping Company, as well as extensive tracts of land. At the time these moves were seen as a first step to taking over the country. In retrospect they appear at least comprehensible in two other senses: firstly, the need of the Soviet economy to recover from its wartime devastation, and secondly, the probability that many – perhaps the bulk – of these reclaimed assets had indeed been taken over by German firms without clear coercion after 1938. Many had received substantial German investment.[34]

In the course of the 1960s, as Austrian neutrality became established, the sense of Soviet threat declined, and a left-wing version of the odyssey gained some currency. In part this extended earlier communist attacks on the Austrian government for being too pro-American, but it was reinforced by a wider 'revisionist' historiography which saw United States 'dollar imperialism' as the main culprit of the Cold War.[35] One target was the rose-tinted interpretation of American Marshall Aid, which had been propagated at the time as that 'most unsordid act' (whether this description was ever seriously believed is another matter). Research showed that in Austria (as elsewhere) there were strong disagreements between the American Economic Co-operation Agency and Austrian domestic interests. But the assumption that the Americans therefore imposed their will on Austrian political élites seems more dubious. And, while the desire of the United States to determine Austrian economic policy on a range of issues is clear,[36] their success in doing so is not. The reorientation of Austrian trade from the Danube to the west, for example, was due to a range of factors (some American experts opposed it because it used rather than saved dollars).[37] The attempts to limit Austrian exports of strategic goods to the east caused much friction with the Austrian authorities. As for the 'politics of productivity', Kurt Tweresar has recently shown the limits of American power when faced by Austrian bureaucrats.[38] Admittedly the actual impact of Marshall Aid on Austria is still something of a *terra incognita* and the history of Austrian reconstruction remains to be written. But it seems unlikely that it will confirm the account of tutelage, any more than the earlier clichés of idealistic generosity. The interactions of American influence with Austria in the cultural sphere, whatever the attraction of the 'American dream', recently explored by Reinhold Wagnleitner, suggest a similarly sceptical conclusion.[39]

The more recent economic revisionism, which suggests that the importance of Marshall Aid has been overstated, has not yet been tested in the Austrian case. But the raw statistics suggest that the impression of the overwhelming importance of Marshall Aid, especially for food imports, fertilizers and later on for electrification, will be confirmed.[40] It seems likely that American aid, including the special treatment given in the European Payments Union, allowed Austria to survive despite its massive trading deficit until it was able to take advantage of the West German economic boom.

In one sense the revisionist interpretation of American policy has flowed into a broader stream – the story of Austrian tutelage under Allied occupation. This was inaugurated by Karl Renner's famous comparison (made in September 1945) of the occupation powers to 'four elephants in a rowing-boat', and his appeal to withdraw the over-large armies from the country. The veteran mayor of Vienna, Karl Seitz, gave it eloquent expression in a closed parliamentary session soon afterwards, when he disputed the right of the occupation authorities to give the Austrians lessons in democracy, an opinion often echoed in the Austrian parliamentary speeches in the following decade.[41] Clearly it was galling that the Allied Commission for Austria should continue to exercise supreme authority, despite political parties, elections and parliamentary debates. The consequent resentment and its symbolic impact should not be ignored. Nevertheless, the term 'tutelage' is misleading for a number of reasons. Firstly it has negative connotations, implying that Allied actions within Austrian society were *per se* illegitimate or at least as inappropriate as keeping an adult in short trousers. But this negative connotation creates problems when Allied interference is judged to be necessary on other grounds. Is it really possible to speak of a beneficial form of 'tutelage'?[42] Secondly, the term overlooks the overlapping interests of occupiers and occupied in many fields. But perhaps most important, it and related terms like 'totale Kontrolle' give a misleading impression of the actual distribution of power between occupation authorities and Austrian élites. In theory the powers of the victorious occupiers may appear extensive, but in practice they were constrained by dependence on Austrian 'collaborators'. They were also, even in the case of the Soviet Union, limited by considerations of public image. On the other side Austrian leaders were well able to delay, block or even reverse Allied intentions. They had resources of local knowledge, connections and patronage at their disposal.

IV

The status of 'permanent neutrality', decided by the Austrian Parliament in October 1955, has become a central part of Austrian national identity. Naturally it has also influenced historical accounts of the preceding decade. In general these accounts have seen the connection between the recovery of sovereignty and neutrality as indissoluble (even if, in legal terms, the declaration was a free act of the Austrian Parliament, performed after sovereignty had been restored and the last occupation soldier had left).[43] In many cases there is a sense of teleology, of a journey *towards* the twin destinations of 1955. Even Gerald Stourzh's magisterial account of the State Treaty does not entirely avoid this impression, as his subtitle 'der Weg zur Neutralität' indicates.[44] A similar assumption underlies the revisionist historiography of the Cold War, which charged Austria's leaders with leaning too far to the West (under American pressure) and thus endangering both neutrality and the chances of agreeing a State Treaty.[45] And the nub of recent disagreements about the role of the vice-chancellor, Adolf Schärf, and Karl Gruber seems to be the question of whether they promoted or hindered advance towards the twin destination of neutrality and sovereignty.[46]

The case for the linkage of neutrality and sovereignty is clear enough in 1955. Soviet agreement to withdraw was conditional on an Austrian commitment to declare its neutrality. But was it in some sense 'latent' in the preceding decade?[47] Before the East–West divide solidified, the question of neutrality had little concrete meaning, and the wish to avoid a one-sided orientation to East or West or the desire to emulate Switzerland were hardly policy statements. Indeed, in two senses Austria stood to gain from the Cold War: firstly, it could move out of its association with Nazi Germany and into the Western camp. The relevant benchmark here, in other words, is not neutrality but the status of a semi-defeated, occupied country. Secondly, as a country apparently under threat of communism, Austria became much more interesting to the United States than it would have done on purely economic grounds.

Yet clearly the division of Europe into two hostile camps also brought dangers. The greatest fear at the time was that the East–West divide would lead to a division of the country, as in the German case. Although there were obvious differences, such as the existence of a functioning Austrian government and the relatively co-operative Allied rule in the capital, these fears were understandable. And there is evidence that the idea of division was circulating among some Western policy-makers in 1947–8, ostensibly as a defensive move against a Soviet threat to the Marshall Plan. But the basic problem of Austria's Western orientation was that it constrained Austria's foreign policy options; above all it virtually ruled out the path of negotiating bilaterally with the Soviet Union.

This was shown on a number of occasions in the diplomacy of the late 1940s, as Gruber urged the Americans to make concessions to the Soviet Union – but with little success. In a sense he was hoisted by this own petard. Having 'entangled' the United States into Austrian affairs by arguing that the country was in danger of falling to communism, he found it difficult to persuade the Americans that concessions could safely be made, and that the Austrians could deal with any future threat.[48] In short Austria's fate was being tied to domestic American politics at a time when the fear in Washington of being accused of being 'soft on communism' made any deal a political risk. The proposal to buy out Soviet claims to German assets (the 'Cherrière plan'), in effect by using American dollars, increased this link even further. For the State Department the important point was that

> nach aussenhin Österreich selbst diesen Betrag an die Sowjetunion überweist, da in der amerikanischen Öffentlichkeit der Eindruck unbedingt vermieden werden müsse, daß die Sowjetunion amerikanische Steuergelder in irgend einer Form erhält.[49]

> (ostensibly Austria herself is to transfer the sum to the Soviet Union since at all costs the impression must be avoided with the American public that the Soviet Union is receiving American taxes in any form whatever.)

The same fear of public opinion led to a stiffening of the
American position in the summer of 1949, after the four occupying powers had apparently agreed a treaty in Paris in June.
The Austrian foreign minister could cajole and complain about
this but he knew he had nowhere else to go.

Part of this dependence was economic. Arguments about the
allocation of Marshall Aid and the release of Counterpart funds
were raging between the Americans and the Austrian officials.[50]
Now the Austrian Cabinet was worried that, if it offered concessions in the treaty negotiations without American agreement,
'durch eventuelle Vestimmung der Amerikaner in weiterer Folge
materieller Schaden, insbesondere Marshall Plan eintreten
könnte' ('by possibly upsetting the Americans material damage,
especially in [respect of] the Marshall Plan, could occur').[51]

But as well as economic dependence there was a dependence
based on fear – the shared perception of a Soviet threat. In the
lapse of time since 1955 this point has become neglected and
tends to be underplayed in narratives of neutrality. Even if, as
already suggested, the perception was probably incorrect, it did
lead Austrian leaders to look to the West not just for psychological support and economic aid but also for military security, not
excluding membership of the Brussels Treaty Organization and
NATO. For the leadership of the People's Party (ÖVP), this fitted
into their view of Austria as a Western bastion, or as Chancellor
Figl put it, 'the Eastern Fortress of Western Democracy amid a
sea of Communism or potential Communism'.[52] He later related
this to his belief that Russians were aiming at eventual annexation of Vienna 'in the hope of reversing [the] consequences of
[the] historical turning point marked by [the] successful resistance
of Vienna to Turks'(sic!).[53]

Perhaps even more strikingly, the leadership of the SPÖ also
swung round to the belief that Austria should sign the Brussels
Treaty. Inner party opposition based on anti-Americanism and
anti-capitalism or the hope of a 'Third Force' became marginal-
ized, as elsewhere in Western European social democracy.[54]
Schärf at any rate was clear that while Austria was not in a position to join, 'this did not mean that she was not in sympathy with
the objectives of the parties to the [Brussels] treaty'.[55] Soon after
he told the US minister in Vienna that since 'any direct adherence
to [the] Western Bloc would be considered by [the] Soviets as

provocation . . . the Austrian government must "pretend" to be neutral in East–West controversy in order to persuade [the] Soviets to renew treaty negotiations but . . . this policy is purely tactical as Austrian socialists [are] fully aware that future economic, political and military support must come from [the] West'.[56] He later indicated to the French socialist Léon Blum, 'daß wir die Einordnung in ein größeres politisches und vermutlich auch militärisches System brauchen'('that we need the inclusion into a larger political and presumably also military system').[57] By the early 1950s social democratic leaders developed an almost reflex rejection of what was seen as the communist slogan of neutrality.[58]

Austria's foreign minister, Karl Gruber, who belonged to the People's Party, pursued a policy which was within the bounds of this coalition consensus, albeit at the pro-Western end of the range. Early in 1948 his fears about a potential Soviet threat led him to relegate sovereignty to second place until the Western defence organization had materialized.[59] He hoped 'that Austria would be admitted to the Western Union on conclusion of the Treaty' because 'Austria . . . could not be expected to maintain her independence unless she threw her lot in with the West'.[60] He spoke enthusiastically in Cabinet about the establishment in the West of 'eine große Bewegung, eine Sicherheitsorganisation wegen des russischen Vormarsches und dessen Abstoppung' ('a great movement, a security organization because of the Russian advance and [the question of] stopping it').[61] This and other evidence makes it clear that Gruber assumed that Western rearmament would bring Austria the protection it needed, once sovereignty had been recovered. His suggestion to the British foreign secretary, Ernest Bevin, early in 1949 that Austria's inclusion in the Atlantic Pact 'would be infinitely preferable to the type of Four-Power guarantee set out in the treaty' is therefore not surprising or anomolous.[62] In the *Angst* of the late 1940s neutrality was not a reassuring prospect, much less a foreign policy aim. It meant that, in the words of the Austrian observer in Brussels, 'das kleine Österreich nunmehr eindeutig außerhalb der neuen europäischer Schutzorganisation' ('little Austria is now clearly outside the new European Protection organization') or in a 'no man's land'.[63]

Naturally tactical considerations meant Austria had to think hard about associating with Western European institutions. But a softly-softly approach ('auf sanften Pfoten gehen') should not be elevated into a foreign-policy principle. Neither should the frequent public affirmations by Austrian politicians that they sought to build bridges, to avoid siding with either East or West, or to follow Switzerland's example.[64] State Secretary Ferdinand Graf's expectation of Austria's future membership of NATO in July 1949 appears an aberration (*Extratour*)[65] only in the sense that it published an assumption that had previously been kept outside the public domain.[66] In any case, a point which has generally been overlooked, is that it is by no means clear that the Soviet Union would – or could – have blocked Austrian membership of NATO at this stage. In the late 1940s, when the Soviet Union seemed on several occasions ready to sign a treaty, it failed to make neutrality a condition.

It was only after 1950, when the accusation of a Western orientation was often made by the Soviet Union, and West German rearmament became the main point of contention between East and West, that Soviet opposition to Austria joining Western organizations became more important. When membership of the Council of Europe was urged by some enthusiasts, the government concluded that the benefits of membership hardly offset the disadvantage of annoying the Russians. As Chancellor Figl told his Cabinet in July 1950:

> Österrreich ist noch immer ein von vier Mächten besetztes Land. Deutschland kann nicht zum Vergleich herangezogen werden; es herrschen dort ganz andere Verhältnisse, Westdeutschland kann als eindeutig westlich oriertiert auftreten, weil es ja nur von den westlichen Alliierten besetzt ist. Wir sind ja auch so orientiert, aber wir haben auf unserer Lage Rücksicht zu nehmen; auszukosten hätte die Folgen ja nur die österreichische Bevölkerung und ich sehe nicht ein, warum man sie unnütz einer Schikane aussetzen soll.[67]

> (Austria is still a country occupied by four powers. Germany can not be taken as a comparison; the situation there is quite different. West Germany can show its Western orientation clearly, but we have to consider our position; it would only be the Austrian population which would have to bear the consquences [of membership] and I don't see why they should be unnecessarily exposed to [Soviet] chicanery.)

The Coal and Steel Community was a more difficult calculation since the concrete advantages of membership, such as access to West German and Italian markets and assured supplies of Ruhr coal, seemed clearer. But here, too, fear of Soviet objections to closer links with West Germany led Austria to apply only for observer status before the State Treaty. Nevertheless, neither before nor even after the declaration of neutrality did non-membership seem to have been excluded as a matter of principle.[68]

The changes which put neutrality on the agenda in 1955 have often been described in personal terms, above all in terms of changes in leadership: on the Austrian side the replacement of Leopold Figl as Austrian chancellor by the more pragmatic Julius Raab in April 1953, and, to a lesser extent, the removal of the Austrian foreign minister, Gruber, on the Soviet side, the death of Stalin in March 1953 and the emergence of a new foreign policy under Khruschev. Obviously these changes should not be ignored. But neither should they divert attention from the changes in the two structural factors which had constrained Austria in the 1940s and early 1950s, the shared perception of a Soviet threat, and economic dependence on the USA.

The first change was not a linear process. After the Korean War Austrian security worries probably increased and links with the United States (and to a lesser extent with France and Britain) over training and equipping the paramilitary 'B-Gendarmerie' intensified. In this period Austria has been called 'something like a secret ally of the west'.[69] Once the Korean War scare had subsided, the need for Western protection became less self-evident; indeed it may have become clear to the Austrians that it rested on a Western assumption of an indefinite occupation of Austria. Furthermore, even without incessant Soviet warnings about Austria's incorporation into the European Defence Community, the prospect of fighting side by side with German soldiers was probably unacceptable to Austrians. Nevertheless, even in 1955, serious reservations about the status of neutrality were expressed by Adolf Schärf. These were partly based on the fear of 'neutralization', which was seen as a softening-up process for communist domination. Behind this there was still a residual fear of Soviet intentions. At best, neutrality appeared a leap in the dark. For this reason Bruno Kreisky (then state secretary for foreign affairs) told Western ambassadors in 1956 that it would be useful if the

terms of any guarantee for Austria went beyond the terms of the
United Nations charter to 'have the effect of bringing NATO to
Austria's aid quickly if she were attacked from the East'.[70] In the
years after 1955 there developed, despite neutrality, what Oliver
Rathkolb describes as a *de facto* military alliance with NATO in
case of overall war'. It was only in 1958 during the Lebanon crisis
that neutrality began to assume its later form, when it was
asserted against American overflights of Austrian territory.[71]

In economic relations Austria gained greater freedom of
manœuvre with the end of Marshall Aid and the improvement in
her trading position at the end of 1952. Now for the first time
Austria's balance of payments was in the black, its currency sta-
bilized and its budget balanced.[72] It was surely no coincidence
that in April 1953 the Austrian government told Western governments that it now did not 'anticipate any difficulty in meeting
[its] obligations to buy out the Soviet claim to German assets'.[73]
American dislike of doing a deal with the Soviet Union may not
have lessened as the Republicans took over in Washington, but
the Austrian need to defer to it did. Shortly afterwards the
Austrian government showed that it was prepared to risk
Western displeasure by using Indian mediation to explore the
possibility of Austrian neutrality as a route to Soviet concessions.
Even though this did not produce the hoped-for response, it did
prefigure the situation in 1955 when the Austrian government
ignored Western misgivings, flew to Moscow and agreed a for-
mula on neutrality despite deep reservations in the West. It is hard
to imagine that the Austrians would have been able or willing to
act so independently five years earlier.

V

Variants or combinations of the three benign narratives became
established in Austrian historiography in the two-and-a-half
decades which followed the State Treaty, reaching a symbolic
high point in 1980 with the celebration of the twenty-fifth
anniversary of the State Treaty.[74] It would be wrong to suggest
that criticism and self-criticism were wholly missing, but they
were often the work of outsiders swimming 'against the stream',
like Friedrich Heer. The educational narrative allowed, almost by
definition, only a limited amount of self-criticism. The odyssey

narrative implied that the prolonged occupation was essentially unwarranted, and denazification was an act of Allied tutelage which in part violated basic legal principles.[75] In accounts of Austria's escape from communism the Nazi legacy was important essentially because it could be exploited by the Soviet Union and the Austrian communists.[76] Accounts of the Austrian Treaty negotiations also tended to ignore or veil connections with the immediately preceding period; the reference to Austria's 'responsibility' in the Treaty preamble, for example, was seen as an almost self-evident injustice, its removal in 1955 as a confirmation of the rightfulness of the Austrian case.[77] The dispute over German external assets was seen as the result either of Soviet rapaciousness or of the inability of the Great Powers to agree a complex technical question, but certainly not of any Austrian involvement in the German war effort. Similarly, restitution was seen largely as a matter of Western companies (above all, oil firms) seeking Austrian resources; 'arianized' property was hardly mentioned.[78] (The same lacunas are evident in the official selection of American documents, *The Foreign Relations of the United States*).[79]

Two works of the 1980s exemplify the problems of fitting awkward subjects into the benign narratives. Dieter Stiefel's study of denazification adopts the education narratives, by stating that 'Eine Entnazifizierung im Sinne einer Abwendung der Bevölkerung vom Nationalsozialismus war bis zum Kriegsende schon weitgehend erfolgt' ('a denazification in the sense of the population turning away from National Socialism had to a great extent already happened by the end of the war'). If denazification was necessary at all it was largely for foreign relations reasons, to conform to Allied requirements or to accommodate the emotional needs of the victims. It soon gave way to inevitable reintegration and (necessary) taboo, and in the end contributed to Austria's 'inneren Befriedigung' ('domestic pacification'). In overall sociological terms, Stiefel concluded, it confirmed and regulated changes in élites and ownership structures which had been happening since the monarchy. What is interesting here is not just the thin empirical base of the argument (including a naïve acceptance of denazification statistics) but also the stance of the dispassionate, disengaged observer, standing above the historical fray.[80]

Hugo Portisch's mammoth television project, *Österreich II*
(twenty-four broadcasts of ninety minutes each!) adopted a
rather more didactic role but, like Stiefel, his basic assumption
was that the Austrians had learnt a lesson from National
Socialism. The problem, as Portisch saw it, was that the occupying powers came along (and with them the victims) and, albeit
for understandable reasons, nipped the healthy process of
learning in the bud: 'Denn man fragte nicht nach dem
Lernprozeß, man fragte nach der Mitschuld. Die Frage stoppte
den Lernprozeß' ('for people were no longer asked about the
educational process but about their share of guilt. The question
stopped the education.') This assumption about the state of mind
of the Austrian population in 1945 was based on the impression
gained from conversations with Austrians in the 1980s.[81] But the
main point is its implication that continuity of anti-Semitism or
the post-war strength of ex-Nazis could be ascribed to excessive
Allied interference. The rest of the series presents almost all the
permutations of the odyssey, tutelage and neutrality narratives in
self-indulgent detail. Despite its appearance of pioneering didac-
ticism, it remained firmly within the bounds of the benign narrative. Not surprisingly it was a considerable success.

While *Österreich II* was being broadcast, Austrian politics
became involved in polemical controversies about the Nazi past.
Political events such as the welcome given to the returning war
criminal, Walter Reder, by the defence minister, Frischenschlager,
and, above all, Kurt Waldheim's disputed revelations of his military service during the Second World War clearly acted as trig-
gers.[82] There was also a left–right political divide involved: in
general the critical narrative was a continuation of earlier communist and 'new left' narratives but largely shorn of their Austrian patriotism. In some cases this led to a switch from traditional left-wing, anti-Prussian positions to something bordering
on admiration for the supposedly superior way West Germany
had 'coped with' its Nazi past. Above all the critical narrative
was a generational conflict and a reaction to what were seen as
the deficiencies and conscious suppressions of post-war politics.

Within this critical narrative two broad lines can be distinguished: the first was the view of the *Anschluß* not as an aberration but as part of an Austrian tradition going back to the
monarchy. Austrian treatment of Slav minorities was one aspect

of this, seen not as more benign and tolerant than that of the Prussians, but as an expression of 'Austrian German national' racial superiority.[83] Above all, Austrian anti-Semitism moved to centre stage. Previously it had often been included in the educational package almost *en passant*, as in the assumption in Erich Zöllner's standard history that 'Auch die immer mehr verschärften Maßnahmen gegen die Juden, . . . wurden durch die große Mehrzahl der Bevölkerung abgelehnt' ('the increasingly severe measures against the Jews . . . were also rejected by the great majority of the population').[84] Critics like Erika Weinzierl or Albert Massiczeck were isolated voices. In the critical narratives, by contrast, anti-Semitism appeared as part of an indigenous tradition and Nazi treatment of the Jews was seen as not merely having been accepted by the population but encouraged or anticipated by it.[85] The educational narrative was undermined by post-war evidence, not only of anti-Semitism in the 1986 presidential election campaign but also in Cabinet discussions in the immediate post-war period. These showed that even where ministers did not express anti-Semitism themselves they showed little readiness to take political risks by confronting it within society.[86]

A second strand in the critical narrative focuses more on the post-war period, and often implies that somewhere an opportunity was missed. In some accounts American policy was blamed for its shift away from the policy of élite exchange towards mobilizing against communism.[87] More recently the emphasis has been placed on resistance from within Austrian society. Attention has turned on the way the history and memories of National Socialism have been selectively conveyed in families, schools and even by historians.[88]

The clash between the older narratives and the more recent critical one is as much about sensibility as about facts. This can be seen both in the sense of outrage of some of the critical narratives and in the irritation with which criticism, with or without outrage, is received. Gerd Bacher's introduction to the second volume of *Österreich II*, for example, sees the critical narrative as the 'wrong' sort of way of dealing with the Nazi past, one based on moralizing and 'Besserwisserei'. The right sort, he suggests, is one which encourages dialogue between generations and could be accepted by the bulk of the population. His suggestion is that enlightenment into painful problems is necessary but it should be done without causing pain. The charge of moralizing has also recently been revived by Gabriele Holzer, who charges adherents of what she calls the 'Gnadenlose Gute' ('Goodness without mercy') with both exaggeration and a kind of political correctness.[89]

Naturally, moral indignation is not enough. But the suggestion that moralizing, in the sense of making moral judgements, can be avoided when the Third Reich is discussed is either naïve or disingenuous. The benign narratives themselves involve a series of such judgements and a selection of facts in accordance with them. This selective version of the past cannot simply incorporate less palatable revelations and conclude that 'there was no alternative'. In short there is a problem in switching from a position that nothing much objectionable happened to the view that those objectionable things which happened were unavoidable.

Where the critical narrative undoubtedly could be extended is in exploring the nature and extent of constraints on Austria's development. There are, after all, many different forms of 'inevitability'. For example, it makes a considerable difference if denazification was thwarted by the effects of the Cold War and shifts in American policy, or if it was an impossible enterprise from the start. Similarly, even if a reintegration of National Socialists was 'functionally necessary' for Austrian society, does it follow that the reintegration needed to take place in the manner it did? As for the question of anti-Semitism, it is important to decide whether politicians were identifying with popular attitudes or reluctantly bowing to them.[90] On the issue of redress to Nazi victims, a continuing source of controversy, it clearly makes a difference if claims were rejected as a matter of legal logic – based on the view that Austria herself had been a victim – as a consequence of administrative problems due to the sheer complexity of the material, or as a result of political pressure.[91] Contrary to some assumptions, restitution (unlike reparation) did not involve an admission of legal responsibility for 'arianization' and thus was not rendered impossible by the 'victim thesis'.

VI

In exploring the implications and addressing some of the problems of these four accounts of post-war Austria, I do not want to suggest that they should or could simply be discarded. But a consciousness of their influence on the basic assumptions of Austrian historiography may lead to greater awareness of problems in interpreting these writers. For, as the recent and welcome liberalization of archival policy shows, more archival sources do not *ipso facto* mean more useful knowledge, though they will certainly produce more publications. What I have tried to suggest here is one way in which the assumptions with which historians examine new documents can themselves be usefully scrutinized.

Notes

[1] See Gordon Brook-Shepherd, *The Austrian Odyssey* (London, 1957); Fritz Molden, *Die Österreicher oder die Macht der Geschichte* (Munich, 1986).

[2] Erika Weinzierl, 'Vor- und Frühgeschichte der Zweiten Republik', in Anton Pelinka and Rolf Steininger (eds.), *Österreich und die Sieger: 40 Jahre 2. Republik – 30 Jahre Staatsvertrag* (Vienna, 1986), pp. 109–30.

[3] Ernst Hanisch, *Der lange Schatten des Staates, Österreichische Geschichte im 20. Jahrhundert* (Vienna, 1994), pp. 389–94.

[4] Robert Keyserlingk, *Austria in World War II: An Anglo-American Dilemma* (Kingston and Montreal, 1988), p. 160.

[5] *Rot–Weiss–Rot Buch. Gerechtigkeit für Österreich! (nach amtlichen Quellen)*, vol. 1 (Vienna, 1946); see also the criticism by the basically sympathetic Brook-Shepherd in *The Austrian Odyssey*, p. 142.

[6] Robert Knight, 'Besiegt oder Befreit? Eine völkerrechtliche Frage historisch betrachtet', in Günter Bischof and Josef Leidenfrost (eds.), *Die Bevormundete Nation: Österreich und die Alliierten 1945–1950* (Innsbruck, 1988), pp. 75–92, 357.

[7] Dieter Binder, 'The Second Republic: Austria seen as a continuum', *Austrian History Yearbook*, 26 (1995), pp. 19–21.

[8] Kabinettsrat, 19th session, 24 July 1945, Archiv der Republik, Vienna [AdR].

[9] Cited in Robert Knight, 'Education and national identity in Austria after the Second World War', in Ritchie Robertson and Edward Timms (eds.), *The Habsburg Legacy: National Identity in Historical Perspective* (Austrian Studies 5, Edinburgh, 1994), pp. 186–7.

[10] Karl Stadler, *Österreich 1938–1945, im Spiegel der NS Akten* (Vienna, 1966), p. 10.

[11] Fred Parkinson (ed.), *Conquering the Past: Austrian Nazism Yesterday and Today* (Detroit, 1989), pp. 11–13.

[12] See Wolfgang Muchitsch (ed.), *Österreicher im Exil: Großbritannien 1938–1945* (Vienna, 1992); Ernst Buschbeck, *Austria* (London, 1949), pp. 147 ff.

[13] Felix Kreissler, *Der Österreicher und seine Nation. Ein Lernprozeß mit Hindernissen* (Vienna, 1984).

[14] Felix Kreissler, 'Die Bedeutung der Österreichischen Emigration bis 1945', in Pelinka and Steininger (eds.), *Österreich und die Sieger*, p. 20.

[15] For a recent overview, see Evan Bukey, 'Nazi rule in Austria', *Austrian History Yearbook*, 23 (1992), 202–33; see also Charlie Jeffery, 'Konsens und Dissens im Dritten Reich', *Zeitgeschichte* 19, 5/6 (Mai/Juni 1992), 129–47.

[16] Adolf Schärf, *Österreichs Erneuerung 1945–1955. Das erste Jahrzehnt der Zweiten Republik* (7th edn, Vienna, 1955), p. 24.

[17] See, for example, Manfried Rauchensteiner, *Die Zwei: Die Große Koalition in Österreich 1945–1966* (Vienna, 1987), p. 20, though he still believes that in 1943 'suddenly the realization came that a false idea had been chased and false leaders had been followed'.

[18] Josef Schöner, *Wiener Tagebuch 1944/1945*, ed. Eva-Marie Csáky (Vienna, 1992), pp. 46–7; see also Evan Bukey, 'Popular opinion in Vienna after the Anschluß', in Parkinson, *Conquering the Past*, pp. 151–64.

[19] See John Bernbaum, '"The new elite" Nazi leadership in Austria, 1938–1945', *Austrian History Yearbook*, 14 (1978), 145–88.

[20] See Hans Witek and Hans Safrian, *Und keiner war dabei. Dokumente des alltäglichen Antisemitismus* (Vienna, 1988).

[21] Bukey, 'Popular opinion', p. 156.

[22] Ibid., pp. 154–5.

[23] Alfred Ableitinger, 'Die innenpolitische Entwicklung', in Wolfgang Mantl (ed.), *Politik in Österreich: Die Zweite Republik, Bestand und Wandel* (Vienna, 1992), p. 119; Hanisch, *Der lange Schatten*, p. 397; Emmerich Tálos, 'Sozialpartnerschaft. Ko-operation – Konzertierung – politische Regulierung', in Herbert Dachs *et al.* (eds.), *Handbuch des politischens Systems* (Vienna, 1991), pp. 391–2.

[24] Dieter Binder, 'The Second Republic: Austria seen as a continuum', *Austrian History Yearbook*, 26 (1995), p. 19.

[25] Binder's account (in ibid., pp. 42–3), of post-war democracy hardly accounts for the phenomena he criticizes so vehemently, like anti-Semitism.

[26] Michael Gehler, '"Die Besatzungsmächte sollen schnellstmöglich nach Hause gehen." Zur österreichischen Interessenpolitik des Außenministers Karl Gruber 1945–1953', *Christliche Demokratie*, 1 (1994), 27–78.

27 Knight, 'Besiegt'; Günter Bischof, 'Die Instrumentalisierung der Moskauer Erklärung nach dem 2. Weltkrieg', *Zeitgeschichte*, 20, 11/12 (November/December 1993), 345–66.

28 See chapter six of Gerald Stourzh's *Geschichte des Staatsvertrages 1945–1955, Österreichs Weg zur Neutralität* (Graz, 1985); see also Charles Yost, 'Concluding observations', in Robert Bauer (ed.), *The Austrian Solution: International Conflict and Co-operation* (Charlotteville, 1982), p. 205.

29 Minsterrat 247, 247th session, 8 May 1951, Archiv der Republik, Vienna [AdR].

30 William Stearman, *The Soviet Union and the Occupation of Austria: An Analysis of Soviet Policy in Austria 1945–1955* (Bonn, 1962); see also Gerald Stourzh, 'The origins of Austrian neutrality', in Alan T. Leonhard (ed.), *Neutrality. Changing Concepts and Practices* (Lanham, 1988), pp. 52–3.

31 Brook-Shepherd, *The Austrian Odyssey*, pp. 6–7.

32 See Wilfried Aichinger, *Die Sowjetische Österreichpolitik 1943–5* (Vienna, 1977), pp. 190ff.

33 See Michael Ludwig, Klaus Dieter Mulley and Robert Streibel (eds.), *Der Oktoberstreik 1950. Ein Wendepunkt der Zweiten Republik* (Vienna, 1991).

34 Robert Knight (ed.), *Ich bin dafür, die Sache in die Länge zu ziehen: Die Wortprotokolle der Bundesregierung über die Wiedergutmachung der Juden 1945–1952* (Frankfurt am Main, 1988), pp. 40–1.

35 See Arno Einwitschläger, *Amerikanische Wirtschaftspolitik in Österreich 1945–1949* (Vienna, 1986).

36 Wilfried Mähr, *Der Marshall-plan in Österreich* (Graz, 1989); see also David Ellward, *Rebuilding Western Europe: America and Postwar Reconstruction* (London, 1992).

37 See Gerhard Rosegger, 'East–West trade: the Austrian example 1945–1958', *Journal of Central European Affairs*, 22 (1962), 79–95.

38 Kurt Tweraser, 'The policies of productivity and corporatism: the late Marshall Plan in Austria, 1950–1954', in Günter Bischof (ed.), *Austria in the Nineteen Fifties* (Contemporary Austrian Studies 3, Innsbruck, 1995), pp. 91–9.

39 Reinhold Wagnleitner, *Coca-Colonisation und Kalter Krieg. Die Kulturmission der USA in Österreich nach dem Zweiten Weltkrieg* (Vienna, 1991).

40 Probably the best account is Felix Butchek, *Die österreichische Wirtschaft im 20. Jahrhundert* (Stuttgart, 1985), p. 90; see also Alan Milward, *The Reconstruction of Western Europe, 1945–1950* (London, 1984), p. 103.

41 Manfried Rauchensteiner, *Der Sonderfall: die Besatzungszeit in Österreich 1945–1955* (Graz, 1979), pp.165–6.

[42] See for example Siegfried Beer, 'Die Briten und das Schul- und Bildungswesen in der Steiermark 1945–1947', in Bischof and Leidenfrost (eds.), *Die Bevormundete Nation*, pp. 155–86.

[43] Edwin Loebenstein, '40 Jahre Republik Österreich – 30 Jahre Staatsvetrag', in Pelinka and Steininger, *Österreich und die Sieger*, p. 148.

[44] Stourzh, *Geschichte*, p. 98.

[45] Hanns Haas, 'Österreich 1949: Staatsvertragsverhandlungen und Wiederbewaffnungsfrage', in *Jahrbuch für Zeitgeschichte* (Vienna, 1978), pp. 175–200.

[46] Gehler, 'Besatzungsmächte', 27–78; idem, introduction to *Karl Gruber – Reden und Dokumente 1945–1953* (Vienna, 1994); Günter Bischof, 'The making of a Cold Warrior': Karl Gruber and Austrian foreign policy, 1945–1953', *Austrian History Yearbook*, 26 (1995), 99–127.

[47] Stourzh, *Geschichte*, p. 98.

[48] See Robert Knight, 'British policy towards Occupied Austria 1945–1950' (unpublished University of London Ph.D. thesis, 1986).

[49] Platzer Minute, 27 July 1949, Alfons Schilcher (ed.), *Österreich und die Großmächte. Dokumente zur österreichischen Außenpolitik 1945–1955* (Vienna, 1980), document 59.

[50] Mähr, *Der Marshall-plan*, pp. 190ff.

[51] Figl to Gruber, 23 August 1949, AdR, BMfAA pol-49, Staatsvertrag 3 (telegram no. 59966).

[52] Mack to Foreign Office (FO), 15 March 1946, Public Record Office (PRO), FO371/55284/C2924.

[53] Rendel to FO, 5 June 1947, PRO, FO371/64089/C7777.

[54] Martin Hehemann, '"Daß einzelne Genossen darüber erschreckt sind, daß wir kategorisch jedwede Teilnahme an der EWG ablehnten": Die SPÖ und die Anfänge der europäischen Integration 1945–1959', in Michael Gehler and Rolf Steininger (eds.), *Österreich und die europäische Integration 1945–1993* (Vienna, 1993), pp. 327–45.

[55] Cheetham to Dean, 26 March 1948, PRO, FO371/70408/C2683.

[56] Erhardt to Marshall, 3 June 1948, *Foreign Relations of the United States 1948, II* (Washington, 1973); Stourzh, *Geschichte*, p. 103.

[57] Karl Stadler, *Adolf Schärf: Mensch, Politiker, Staatsmann* (Vienna, 1982), p. 377; Oliver Rathkolb, 'Austria and European integration after World War II', in Günter Bischof and Anton Pelinka (eds.), *Austria in the New Europe* (Contemporary Austrian Studies, 1, New Brunswick/London, 1993), p. 44.

[58] Günter Bischof, 'The making of a Cold Warrior'.

[59] Knight, 'British policy', 178ff.

[60] Marjoribanks Minute, 20 February 1948, PRO, FO371/70395/C1453.

[61] Ministerratsprotokoll (MRP) 106, 6 April 1948, AdR.

[62] See Knight, 'British policy', 225ff.; Günter Bischof, 'Österreich – ein "geheimer Verbündeter" des Westens? Wirtschafts- und sicherheits-

politische Fragen der Integration aus der Sichte der USA', in Gehler and Steininger (eds.), *Österreich und die europäische Integration*, p. 435.

63 Ludwig Report, 7 March 1949, Buresch Minute, 17 March 1949 AdR, BMfAA/ pol-49/ International/ 80.108–81.839.

64 Florian Weiss, 'Die Schwierige Balance: Österreich und die Anfänge der westeuropäischen Integration 1947–1959', *Vierteljahresheft für Zeitgeschichte* (1994); Mähr, *Der Marshall-plan*, pp. 87–91.

65 Stourzh, *Geschichte*, p. 108.

66 Gehler, 'Besatzungsmächte', p. 69, n. 74.

67 MRP 213, 25 July 1950, AdR; see Robert Knight, 'Austrian neutrality and European integration: the historical background', in Karl Koch (ed.), *Austria's Contribution towards European Union Membership* (Guildford, 1995), pp. 28–47; Bischof, 'Geheimer Verbündeter', pp. 435–6.

68 Florian Weiss, 'Die Schwierige Balance', 71–94.

69 Gerald Stourzh, 'The origins of Austrian neutrality', pp. 35–57.

70 Meeting with Western ambassadors, 26 April 1956, PRO, FO371/ 124097/ RR1071/88.

71 Oliver Rathkolb, 'Austria's "Ostpolitik" in the 1950s and 1960s: honest broker or double agent?', *Austrian History Yearbook*, 26 (1995), 144.

72 Felix Butschek, *Die Österreichische Wirtschaft*, p. 1.

73 FO Note, 20 April 1953, PRO, FO371/ 103761/ CA9.

74 See Bundesministerium für Wissenschaft und Forschung *et al.* (eds.), *25 Jahre Staatsvertrag* (4 vols., Vienna, 1980).

75 E.g. (though expressing some doubts about treatment of war crimes) Rudolf Neck, 'Innenpolitische Entwicklung', in Erika Weinzierl and Kurt Skalnik (eds.), *Österreich – die Zweite Republik* (Graz, 1972), p. 159; Gerhard Jagschitz, 'Der Einfluß der alliierten Besatzungsmächte auf die österreichische Strafgerichtsbarkeit von 1945 bis 1955', in *Justiz und Zeitgeschichte: 25 Jahre Staatsvertrag. Protokolle des wissenschaftlichen Symposions* (Vienna, 1981), pp. 114–32.

76 E.g. William Bader, *Austria between East and West, 1945–1955* (Stanford, 1966).

77 Manfred Rauchensteiner, 'Österreich nach 1945 – Der Weg zum Staatsvertrag', in Pelinka and Steininger, *Österreich und die Sieger*, p. 152.

78 See from quite different positions Gerald Stourzh, *Geschichte*, p. 30, and Reinhold Wagnleitner, 'Walter Wodak in London 1947 oder die Schwierigkeit, Sozialist und Diplomat zu sein', in Gerhard Botz, Hans Hautmann, Helmut Konrad, Josef Weidenholzer (eds.), *Bewegung und Klasse. Studien zur österreichischen Arbeitergeschichte* (Vienna, 1978), pp. 217–42. One prominent exception is Anton Pelinka, *Windstille: Klagen über Österreich* (Vienna, 1985).

[79] A possible explanation may be that its editorial guidelines require publication of correspondence with foreign governments to be cleared with the government concerned.

[80] Dieter Stiefel, *Entnazifizierung in Österreich* (Vienna, 1981), p. 328.

[81] Hugo Portisch, *Österreich II: Die Wiedergeburt unseres Staates* (Vienna, 1985), p. 28.

[82] See Richard Mitten, *The Politics of Anti-Semitic Prejudice: The Waldheim Phenomenon in Austria* (Boulder, 1992); Sebastian Meissl, Klaus Dieter Mulley and Oliver Rathkolb (eds.), *Verdrängte Schuld – Verfehlte Sühne. Entnazifizierung in Österreich* (Vienna, 1986); Heide-Marie Uhl, *Zwischen Versöhnung und Verstörung. Eine Kontroverse um Österreichs historische Identität fünfzig Jahre nach dem 'Anschluß'* (Vienna, 1992); Anton Pelinka and Erika Weinzierl (eds.), *Das Große Tabu: Österreichs Umgang mit seiner Vergangenheit* (Vienna, 1987); Emmerich Tálos, Ernst Hanisch, Wolfgang Neugebauer (eds.), *NS-Herrschaft in Österreich 1938–1945* (Vienna, 1988).

[83] Karl Stuhlpfarrer and Hanns Haas, *Österreich und seine Slowenen* (Vienna, 1977); Karl Stuhlpfarrer and Siegfried Mattl, 'Abwehr und Inszenierung im Labyrinth der zweiten Republik', in Tálos *et al.* (eds.), *NS-Herrschaft*, pp. 601–24; Walter Manoschek, *'Serbien ist Judenfrei' Militärische Besatzunspolitik und Judenvernichtung in Serbien 1941/2* (Munich, 1993).

[84] Erich Zöllner, *Geschichte Österreichs von den Anfängen bis zur Gegenwart* (3rd edn, Munich, 1966), p. 526.

[85] Witek and Safrian, *Und keiner war dabei.*

[86] Mitten, *Politics of Anti-Semitic Prejudice*; Robert Knight, *'Ich bin dafür'.*

[87] Oliver Rathkolb, 'US-Entnazifizierung zwischen kontrollierter Revolution und Elitenrestauration (1945–1949)', *Zeitgeschichte*, 11, 9–10 (1984), 302–25.

[88] Meinrad Ziegler and Waltraud Kannonier-Finster, *Österreichisches Gedächtnis: über Erinnern und Vergessen der NS-Vergangenheit* (Vienna, 1993); Peter Malina and Gustav Spann, 'Der Nationalsozialismus im österreichischen Geschichtslehrbuch, in Tálos *et al.* (eds.), *NS-Herrschaft*, pp. 577–600; Gerhard Botz, '"Eine neue Welt, warum nicht eine neue Geschichte?" Österreichische Zeitgeschichte am Ende ihres Jahrhunderts', in *Österreichische Zeitschrift für Geschichtswissenschaften*, 1 no. 3 (1990), 49–96; Thomas Angerer, 'An incomplete discipline: Austrian *Zeitgeschichte* and recent history', in Bischof and Pelinka (eds.), *Austria in the New Europe*.

[89] Gabriele Holzer, *Verfreundete Nachbarn: Österreich–Deutschland – ein Verhältnis* (Vienna, 1995); cf. Molden, *Österreicher oder die Macht der Geschichte*, pp. 286ff.

[90] See Gehler, 'Besatzungsmächte', 42.

[91] Stiefel, 'Entnazifizierung', p. 58.

3

Doderer's Habsburg Myth:
History, the Novel and National Identity

ANDREW BARKER

In 1957 Heimito von Doderer (1896–1966) was awarded the 'Großer Staatspreis' of the Second Republic for his services to Austrian literature. This accolade signalled the ultimate recognition by the Austrian state of a man who in 1929 had noted approvingly the sentiments of his mentor, Paris Gütersloh, in a letter to the publisher Rudolf Haybach. Gütersloh boasted:

> Ich glaube nur, daß wir, ausgehend die Malerei und Literatur zu ordnen, den österreichischen Staat stürzen werden.[1]

A decade later, Doderer's own correspondence with Gütersloh leaves little doubt that both writers welcomed the *Anschluß* in 1938. Soon after the event, Gütersloh sent Doderer a poem entitled '13. März 1938 zur Befreiung Österreichs und Südtyrols' beginning:

> Nun steigt in allen Wurzeln deutsches Blut!
> Der ganze Garten wieder blutwarm ruht!

The accompanying letter ends with 'Ich grüße Sie mit: Heil Hitler!'[2]

Although Doderer had thought better of his enthusiasm for Hitler's Germany as early as 1940, his problematic past meant that between 1946 and 1950 he was forbidden to publish his works. During this period of proscription, with the Austrian state once more a reality, he set about examining the essence both of totalitarianism (in the essay 'Sexualität und totaler Staat')[3] and of a nationhood which he had once been quite willing to abjure. In

1947 the reborn Austrian wrote in the essay 'Rosa chymica austriaco-hispanica. Voraussetzungen österreichischer Lyrik':

> Die österreichische Nationalität ist die von allen am wenigsten materielle. Sie ist ein Zustand, ein goldener Schnitt nur zwischen Distanzen und Kräften, aus dem man fallen kann, wenn man eine rohe und ungeschickte Bewegung macht. (WdD 232)

The final clause, we may assume, is Doderer's oblique acknowledgement of what had most recently happened to Austrian nationhood when tempted by the blandishments of National Socialism. Seven years later, in 1954, he repeated this formulation verbatim in an unpublished essay with the provocative title 'Der Anschluß ist vollzogen'. By now, prior to the publication of *Die Dämonen* but with the success of *Die Strudlhofstiege* behind him, Doderer's rehabilitation was complete. A further decade on, when delivering an updated, French-language version of this ten-year-old essay in Athens, in a country which had been far from untouched by the attentions of the Third Reich, he spoke not just as the Second Republic's foremost novelist but as a mouthpiece for the new Austria which was trying to dissociate itself from its recent Hitlerian past quite as strenuously as, and probably rather more successfully than, the German Democratic Republic.[4]

In both these successor states to Nazi Germany, the GDR and Austria, the rapid creation of a new national identity was crucial in the aftermath of a regime which had attached overriding importance to the notion of *Deutschtum*. Not surprisingly, perhaps, when the Athens address was published in German in 1964, the reference to the *Anschluß* had been dropped for something more anodyne.[5] Paradoxically, given its original title, this essay could hardly be bettered as the articulation of a particular post-1945 version of Austrianness. As the brief quotation above may suggest, the essay's emphasis is on positive but abstract qualities which outweigh the somewhat veiled acknowledgement of the period 1938–45. These years, which could also be regarded as realizing the dream of German unity for long as popular on the Austrian Left as on the Right, were dismissed by Doderer as 'sieben Jahre unösterreichische Herrschaft' (WdD 241). Austrianness, it would now appear, stood at some arms' length from *Deutschtum*.

Unsurprisingly, Doderer's unspecific, rather evasive version of Austria's most recent past proved alluring to many readers and critics living in an ancient *Kulturnation* which had just been such an intimate player in Hitler's barbarism. It was, of course, no secret that the *Hausdichter* of the Second Republic had, like numerous other Austrians, himself been party to that barbarism: first through membership of a party seeking to eliminate the very notion of 'Austrianness', and secondly as an officer in the German armed forces which had been instrumental in attempting to impose the National Socialist doctrine upon a recalcitrant world. Doderer's is a vision of Austria which is both sentimental and conciliatory, but it was widely held both within Austria and beyond, and it proved remarkably resilient until the Waldheim scandal forced a root-and-branch reassessment of Austrian identity, history and complicity in the Nazi terror. As recently as 1985 a critic could still review Doderer's relationship with Austria with only fleeting reference to the author's National Socialist past.[6] In literature, it fell to Thomas Bernhard, most memorably in the novel *Auslöschung* (1988), to shatter the cosy ahistoricism of a society largely cocooned in collective fantasy, basking in the after-glow of the Moscow declaration of 1943 which had declared Austria to be the first victim of fascism rather than its cradle.

In the Athens address, which is subtitled 'Von der Wiederkehr Österreichs', Doderer derides the notion of political history as the carrier of national identity while simultaneously declining to debate the subject:

> Immer noch gilt die politische Geschichte eines Landes als dessen eigentliche 'Geschichte'. Hier ist nicht der Ort, zu untersuchen, woher diese starke Übertreibung stammt. (WdD 239)

Whatever its intention, it is plain that such an assertion tended to absolve both writer and readership from any form of collective historical responsibility, such as the 99 per cent 'Ja' to Hitler in the plebiscite following the *Anschluß* of 1938.[7] This attempt to convince a compliant bourgeois post-war readership that political history did not matter was reinforced by Doderer's conviction that individuals were not to be reckoned with as prime movers in history. This, it must be remembered, was written less than ten years after the death of Adolf Hitler, and by a trained historian.

Doderer's claim that history is something which happens to us –
'Sie passiert uns, wir sind passiv' (WdD 239) – was sweet music
indeed to the ears of those now eagerly subscribing to the notion
of the 'Rape of Austria'.

Having claimed that personal history is more 'real' than political history, and that individuals are passive victims, Doderer
then protests, not entirely convincingly, that 'real' life actually
happens independently of history:

> Das eigentliche Leben geschieht heute [. . .] unglaublicherweise
> noch immer, ja erst recht, ohne Zusammenhang mit ihr, es geht
> beinahe trotz ihrer weiter [. . .] Wir haben wahrlich keinen Grund
> mehr, 'Geschichte' mit 'politischer Geschichte' gleichzusetzen.
> Und keine Professoren werden das Wesentliche unserer Tage
> aufzeichnen. Vielmehr besorgt das die Romanliteratur. (WdD
> 240)

In the course of this essay I shall look more closely at the historical claims of Doderer's novels in the early 1950s and suggest
that they did little to discourage the propensity of the new Austria
to gloss over as far as possible the Nazi past and evade its citizens' responsibility for acts carried out in the name of that
German state of which 'die Ostmark' had been an integral part.
In the GDR, literature was more formally invoked to underpin a
new national identity, but here the emphasis was laid on a philo-
sophical and political tradition going back many decades which,
it was claimed, had continued to exist alongside fascism. In
effect, it was the notion of a 'good', that is, anti-fascist, Germany
which had been there all along and which had now assumed
nationhood. This nation was one, however, which studiously
avoided the noun Germany in its title and even claimed for itself
a memorial at Auschwitz to the victims of fascism. In Austria,
where memories were also selective and where the 'Grand
Coalition' of the conservative Volkspartei (ÖVP) and the Socialist
Party (SPÖ) was proving both stable and effective, the belief was
encouraged that with the restoration of the Republic 'normal service had been resumed'.

In a speech delivered in Berlin on 18 September 1952, Doderer
even had the temerity to speak of the twelve years of National
Socialism as a time which had not really existed, dubbing it an

Unzeit (WdD 229). This is consistent with his philosophy of the Third Reich being a 'zweite Wirklichkeit', a notion debated at considerable length in his diaries and expressed in the post-war novels.[8] As Doderer himself might have put it, this is not the place to examine in detail the minutiae of his epistemological thought and to deliberate whether a 'second reality' is an unreal reality or a real unreality. However, by claiming that the Hitler years comprised such a 'zweite Wirklichkeit', and that a semblance of reality would only be restored when the regime came to an end, Doderer is insinuating that in some deeper (or higher) sense the recent past did not happen. And indeed, in the section of *Die Dämonen* which is reckoned to be the nearest Doderer came to confronting the *Unzeit* of the Third Reich,[9] the infliction of terror upon innocent victims is unmasked as make-believe, rather than actual torture. This section, revealingly, is set many centuries in the past and is cast in the form of 'rediscovered' late medieval manuscripts, written in Early New High German. It details the pseudo-torment of women accused of witchcraft in the caverns at Neudegg in Carinthia.[10] It would have been scant comfort to any surviving victims of the Third Reich who read Doderer to know that by his analysis their sufferings were only part of a 'second reality', a 'geminderte Wirklichkeit'.

Whereas the leadership in the GDR played up the existence of a 'progressive tradition' in Germany which had finally triumphed with the founding of the First German Workers' and Peasants' State, the Austrian solution was a form of sophistry which in its more extreme guise, as represented by Doderer, considered that the recent past was somehow unreal, and that Austrians were victims rather than perpetrators. From there it would be only a short step to believing that if it had not really happened, then it was nobody's fault, either collectively or individually. It may now become clearer why the *Anschluß* referred to in the original title of the Athens address is nothing as 'unreal' as the events of March 1938; rather it is to be understood as the rejoining of Austria with its own 'true' history. It is the 'Anschluß an die Tiefe der Zeiten' (WdD 244):

> 1945 wurde eine Legalität wiederhergestellt, nämlich die der ersten Republik [. . .] Aber diese Bewegung des Wiederherstellens, welche man 1945 vollzog, blieb nicht auf das eigentlich in's Auge

> gefaßte Objekt beschränkt – nämlich auf die demokratische
> Republik, deren Recht vom Volke ausgeht – sondern es schoß
> dabei gleichsam die ganze Vergangenheit neu zu Kristall; und ein
> unter dem Druck von sieben Jahren unösterreichischer
> Herrschaft verdichtetes österreichisches Bewußtsein bemächtigte
> sich unverzüglich der gesamten und gewaltigen Tradition des
> Landes überhaupt, bis zu den alten Römern hinunter [. . .]
> So ebnete sich die Kerbe von 1918 bedeutend ein. (WdD 241)

The history to which Doderer here subscribes is, of course,
pre-eminently a multi-ethnic one, demonstrating vividly the distance he had travelled since 1 April 1933, the day he joined the
NSDAP (National Socialist German Workers' Party), an officially
proscribed organization in the First Republic. This personal shift
exemplifies the wider phenomenon which the historian Ernst
Brückmüller summed up with admirable concision:

> Der (fast) vollkommenen *Integration* in die deutsche Nation folgte
> nach 1945 die (fast) vollkommene *Flucht* aus ihr. Der nation-
> sbildende gemeinsame Weg war zu Ende, bevor er noch sehr
> weit gegangen war.[11]

In Doderer's case, moreover, he continued to plead for this older,
pluralist (albeit *judenrein*) vision of Austria during the post-1955
years, when Article 7 of the Austrian State Treaty, guaranteeing
the rights of non-German-speaking minorities, was observed
only in the breach:

> Ein situationsbewußter Österreicher jedoch muß heute um jeden
> einzelnen kroatischen oder magyarischen Bauern im Burgen-
> lande, um jeden Slowenen in Südkärnten herzlich froh sein: dies
> aber ganz und gar nicht, um in solchen wertvollen Volksteilen
> eine Art Sprungbrett für irgendwelche Aspirationen zu sehen;
> sondern weil gerade durch jene Mitbürger seinem übernation-
> alen – Nationgefühl ein vertretungsweiser konkreter Anhalt
> geboten wird. (WdD 242f.)[12]

It is not hard to recognize that Doderer, writing after the
Second World War, continues the *schwarz-gelb* tendency in Austrian literature,[13] much as Joseph Roth had done in the late 1920s
and 1930s when faced by the horrors of Hitlerdom. Hence a Jew

from Galicia and a reformed Nazi from Vienna can both be seen as subscribing to what Claudio Magris coined the 'Habsburg Myth' in Austrian letters, that is, the tendency to celebrate a society which existed far more in the imagination of the writer than it had ever done in reality.[14] When examining post-war fiction, and in particular the trilogy made up of *Die erleuchteten Fenster* (1950), *Die Strudlhoftiege* (1951) and *Die Dämonen* (1956), it will become apparent that Doderer's 'österreichische Menschen' are overwhelmingly drawn from precisely those strands of society that helped constitute that myth:

> Offiziere, Adelige und Beamte, daneben aber auch ein gewisses Bürgertum meist jüdischer Herkunkft, das sich in der *Ring-straßengesellschaft* mit jenen anderen Gruppen verbinden konnte. Unterstrichen und besiegelt wurde diese Integration in der Regel durch Nobilitierung und nachfolgende Karriereversuche im nicht-wirtschaftlichen Bereich.[15]

In Doderer's case, by evoking the myth he could effortlessly override inconvenient facts: for example, that probably a majority of German-speaking Austrians fervently desired political and cultural union with Germany both before and after the collapse of the Dual Monarchy. Not for nothing were attempts made to have the First Austrian Republic called Deutsch-Österreich. Luckily for Doderer, however, help is at hand, and he falls gratefully upon an utterance of Paul Valéry, whom he deeply admired, praising the:

> 'Tugenden der deutschen Völker', worunter er etwa Bayern, Schwaben, Österreicher und andere verstanden haben mag, wie man unter den angelsächischen Völkern Engländer, Amerikaner, Kanadier und Australier begreift. (WdD 242)

Having established by means of a revered external authority, and a non-German to boot, that there was no such thing as the German *Volk*, merely *Völker* (just as there was no longer one Reich and one Führer), Doderer's poetic fantasy can now take over to remould the evidence of the recent past: 'Die deutschen Völker sind griechenähnlich; das heißt, sie haben das Prinzip, auf welchem Europa beruht – Mannigfaltigkeit, nicht Einheitlichkeit!

[. . .]' What his Greek audience made of that after their experiences under the jackboot is anybody's guess. Doderer continues:

> Das stark ausgebildete Sein dieser einzelnen Völker verhinderte, wie bei den Griechen, ihre politische Einigung, welche auch bei diesen nur unter Zwang vorübergehend vollzogen wurde, durch eine relativ spät in den griechischen Lebenskreis getretene nördliche Militärmacht: die Makedonier. Tout comme chez nous. (WdD 242)

The essence of this travesty of the political history of German unification under Prussia and the subsequent annexation of Austria into the Third Reich is that National Socialism was an aberration. With sovereign insouciance Doderer simply ignores the inconvenient fact of Hitler's birth in Braunau am Inn. As is the case throughout this most revealing essay, names are never named, momentous dates (such as 1938) are never mentioned. What is truly important is that amongst these German peoples there is one which

> in neuerer Zeit Träger einer übernationalen Großmacht geworden, deren Geschichte sich durch Jahrhunderte mit einem erheblichen Teile der europäischen Geschichte gedeckt hat. Daher ist das wesentlich österreichische Nationalbewußtsein von – übernationaler Struktur. (WdD 242)

What is Austrian is therefore linked not with Austria's acquiescence in German fascism (something which may not have evaded the memory of his Greek audience), but with its imperial past.

In one of the essay's more contrived moments, Doderer now proposes a bizarre version of the collapse of the Empire which, as far as I am aware, is unique to him. Looking back to the end of Empire in 1918, when the various nationalities broke away from the Germanic core, Doderer notes:

> Man hat damit die Existenz Österreichs für wesentlich annulliert gehalten. Man hat keineswegs bedacht, daß jene Mitte sich durch Jahrhunderte derart angereichert und gesättigt hatte mit Influenzen anderer Völker innerhalb der gleichen Staatlichkeit, daß, wäre 1918 nicht gekommen, jene spezifisch österreichische

Art zu existieren – als eines der deutschen Völker, jedoch begabt
mit einer geradezu ungeheuren Assimilations-, ja Integrations-
fähigkeit – wahrscheinlich sehr bald verschwunden wäre, durch
den Verlust seiner idealischen Balance. (WdD 243)

In other words, even if the monarchy had survived, the Germans
were being so swamped by non-Germanic influences in the Dual
Monarchy that their very identity would soon have come under
threat. A not dissimilar argument was put forward by the Nazi
Party to counter what it regarded as the malign influences of
modernism, Jewry and socialism upon the German nation. As far
as Austro-Germans were concerned, however, Doderer believed
that in 1918 an ideal balance had been achieved between the
indigenous capacity for assimilation and the influence of the 'foreign'. Therefore, 'sie zu erhalten, griff 1918 das Schicksal ein, bei
erreichtem Maximum und Optimum'. (WdD 243) The collapse of
the Dual Monarchy had therefore nothing to do with four years
of enervating warfare or the demands of other non-Germanic
peoples for national self-determination. It was nothing less than
an act of benevolent fate, intervening to preserve a special form
of Germanness before it fell prey to disintegration.[16] Swiftly
changing the perspective to modern Austria, Doderer concludes:
'Davon lebt Österreich, und heute noch, daher hat es seinen
großen Namen in der Welt, und mit Recht und als ein legitimer
Erbe.' (WdD 243) By this reckoning, it is as if the years 1918 to
1945, the years of struggle for the rump state which was the First
Republic, and everything that transpired thereafter, had simply
never happened.

In 1955, the year of the *Staatsvertrag* which formally re-established a truly independent Austria, Doderer completed his mammoth novel *Die Dämonen*, a work preceded by its not quite so
bulky 'ramp' *Die Strudlhofstiege* and a related trifle *Die erleuchteten Fenster oder Die Menschwerdung des Amtsrates Julius Zihal.*
These works are important not just for their considerable literary
merits, but because they permit examination of the extent to
which the views on Austrian identity and nationhood expressed
in the Athens address are also given literary expression. They are
equally important in the context of Doderer's view of history.
This, it should be underlined, is not merely the expression
of a dilettante, but of someone who studied history at Vienna

University in the 1920s, and after the war resumed the formal study of the discipline. Significantly, perhaps, he chose to study not modern, but late medieval history, being admitted to the rather exclusive Vienna Institut für Geschichtsforschung in 1950 with a dissertation on Vienna in the Middle Ages. This was real history: in the 'Athener Rede', it will be recalled, he dismisses modern history out of hand as being not the province of academics, but of creative literature.

Of Doderer's 'Vienna trilogy' of the early 1950s, *Die Strudlhof-stiege* has the most recent provenance, being inspired by the author's fond remembrance of that ineffably Viennese locality while serving as a Luftwaffe officer in France. *Die erleuchteten Fenster* was already complete by 1939, by which time, just a year after the *Anschluß*, the author had begun to harbour deep reservations about the course on which the new Germany was embarked. Set exclusively in the latter days of the Habsburg Empire, this novel satirizes the bureaucratic mentality of the civil service but is also a warm and humorous evocation of a society which, despite its imperfections, permitted human growth and happiness. Given Hitler's views on the Austrian Empire it is hardly a surprise that the novel did not see the light of day during the Third Reich. *Die Dämonen*, however, represents the radical rewriting of a novel whose first part was finished in 1936. In those days it was entitled 'Die Dämonen der Ostmark', and it was the work of an author who revelled in the 'purity of his blood' ['Reinheit meines Blutes'].[17]

Written to reveal how Marxism had led to the burning of the Vienna Palace of Justice in 1927, the work was primarily an expression of its author's anti-Semitism, Marxism and Judaism being synonymous in the National Socialist vocabulary:

> Ich glaube, es ist das erste Mal, daß die jüdische Welt im Osten deutschen Lebensraumes von einem rein deutschen Autor in den Versuchsbereich der Gestaltung gezogen wurde. Denn die bisher drüber schrieben [. . .] waren selber Juden und ihre Hervorbringungen können wohl seit langem nicht mehr ernsthaft gelesen werden. Ich versuchte, dieses *Theatricum Judaicum* [. . .] vorzuführen.[18]

In the revised, published version of *Die Dämonen*, however, with the atrocities of the Third Reich an inextinguishable fact, Doderer repudiates the novel's earlier racist intentions when he writes:

> In einer 'rassenreinen' Gesellschaft wird jeder Simpel und Bruta-list, der nicht vorwärtsgekommen ist, mindestens einen 'Arier' vorstellen; die gleiche Auszeichnung kann, bei anders gerich-tetem 'Idealismus', darin liegen, für einen Prolet-arier zu gelten. Dort eine vermeintlichte Gemeinsamkeit der Rasse, hier eine der Klasse, es ist gehupft wie gesprungen. Klassen können ja zu Rassen werden, und umgekehrt. (487)

Anti-Semitism is now derided, but the animus against Marxism remains. This is done in the name of the hostility to all ideologies which Doderer loudly espoused in the post-war years, but which served to mask a deep-rooted conservatism, fully in tune with the artistic realities of an Austria epitomized by the *de facto* ban on Brecht performances at the Burgtheater.

Readers of George Clare's moving memoir *Last Waltz in Vienna* will know that what Doderer felt about Viennese Jews in the 1930s was simply the stock-in-trade of a large segment of opinion in the city.[19] It is intriguing, therefore, to examine his portrayal of Jews in the rewritten version of *Die Dämonen* to see how their portrayal chimes in with his concept of the novelist as the true chronicler of the age, given that the age and society in question was profoundly anti-Semitic. The novel retains a panoply of obviously Jewish characters, as indeed it had to, given its aim of portraying the totality of life as based on Viennese society in the 1920s. The Austria of the early 1950s, whose identity with that of 1918 Doderer was so keen to re-establish, was, however, a country which no longer had the Jewish presence with which he had been on intimate terms, thanks to his first, unhappy marriage to Gusti, daughter of the prominent Jewish physician, Paul Hasterlik.[20] This problematic relationship is addressed in the autobiograph-ical figures of Kajetan von Schlaggenberg and Rene Stangeler and their notably sympathetic Jewish partners, Camy Schedik and Grete Siebenschein. In a manner which suggests compensatory fantasy inspired by a bad conscience, Doderer evokes a vanished world where Jews are not only presented in a more positive light than their gentile fellow citizens, but are granted a level of assimi-lation into non-Jewish society which may strain credulity. It may

also be significant that the portrayal of the Viennese Jewish community is restricted entirely to the acculturated middle classes
and omits mention of the many *Ostjuden* living in the
Leopoldstadt who were not only the butt of Viennese anti-Semites
but also shunned by the more integrated Jewish bourgeoisie. Such
revisionary history did not, however, disturb returning *émigré*
Jews such as Hans Weigel, Hilde Spiel and Friedrich Torberg, who
all approved of Doderer's 'essential decency'.[21] Even a business
shark like Cornel Lasch is portrayed positively, although the chief
financial villain of the piece, and a genuinely unpleasant character, remains the Kammerrat Levielle, né Levi.

Just as Doderer cannot avoid Jewish characters, whom he perhaps tends to idealize, so too there have to be fascists, although
they are never called that. Rather it is within the group dubbed
'die Unsrigen' that we meet the characters 'die [. . .] für das ideol-
ogisch aufgeheizte Klima sorgen',[22] and who now require negative characterization. Thus anti-Semitic figures such as Körger
and Eulenfeld hypocritically accept Jewish hospitality, but in the
one incident in the revised novel where their racist intentions are
openly articulated, they are thwarted by Grete Siebenschein. Out
walking in the Wienerwald, a party separates into groups which
correspond to their racial and political affiliations:

> 'Man marschiert heute sozusagen getrennt', sagte Stangeler [. . .]
> 'in zwei gänzlich gesonderten Gruppen' [. . .]
>   'Fassen Sie dieses getrennte Marschieren sinnbildlich auf, dann
> kommen Sie dem wahren Sachverhalt am nächsten', bemerkte
> (Körger).
>   'Wie – ?' fragte Stangeler.
>   'Von mir aus als die Vision einer besseren Zukunft.'[23]

Grete innocently asks whether she may join the group, to be told
by Körger that she may not. The day is saved when someone gal-
lantly announces that the topic of the conversation is a table-
tennis tournament, whereupon Grete insists it is held at her
house. Doderer thus provides a comforting but trivializing version of the past in which the plans of the Nazis were obstructed.
As Dietrich Weber has remarked of *Die Dämonen* as a whole:

> sie schillern geradezu zwischen Vergangenheit und Gegenwart.
> Spätestens seit man aus Doderers Nachlaß weiß, daß dies Buch

durch die fünfundzwanzig Jahre seiner Entstehungszeit nicht kontinuierlich, sondern weitaus zum größten Teil in den Jahren von 1951 bis 1956 geschrieben wurde, ist es zweifellos nicht richtig zu verstehen, wenn man es eng auf die Zeit seiner Hand-lung in der Vergangenheit der Jahre 1926/27 bezogen sieht und dabei nicht berücksichtigt, daß es zumindest ein Ethos vermittelt, das unmittelbar zur Zeit seines Erscheinens in der Gegenwart der fünfziger Jahre Geltung beansprucht.[24]

In an era anxious to avoid the realities of the past, Doderer's realistically painted portrait of a society where Jews and Gentiles mostly rubbed along well together and in which anti-Semites were obstructed proved beguiling. Whatever impression the pub-lished novel imparts, however, the fact remains that the author's original aim had been to write a work whose intentions were the very opposite of conciliatory. Doderer's objective was to create 'ein großer Zeitroman, der das sozusagen "unterirdische" Werden eines neuen Deutschlands [. . .] in seiner Vorgeschichte zeigen will'.[25] Yet as has been pointed out elsewhere, these intentions turned out differently in practice, for the Jewish characters in 'Die Dämonen der Ostmark' are also portrayed sympathetically, to the dismay of the publishers who turned the novel down, finding 'die Bewältigung des Themas [. . .] nicht profiliert genug, freilich in seinem Sinne, nämlich im nationalsozialisti-schen'.[26]

In keeping with notions outlined in 'Sexualität und totaler Staat', Doderer goes to considerable lengths in Die Dämonen to pinpoint the rise of the Third Reich not in political, sociological, economic or cultural terms (in a combination of which factors most historians would find its genesis), but rather in the sexual malpractices of the characters. For example, the preference of the autobiographical Kajetan von Schlaggenberg for large women is intimately linked with his anti-Semitism, which surfaces after the breakdown of his marriage to the slim, Jewish, Camy Schedik. This goes to the autobiographical heart of Die Dämonen, whose original working title in the early 1930s was the similarly alliera-tive 'Dicke Damen'. At this time Doderer's own marriage foundered, and it is known that he himself had a penchant for fat (Jewish) women with whom he could indulge in the (mock) sado-masochistic torture of the type portrayed in the caverns at Neudegg. In this instance, the pre-war notion of the '"unterir-disches Werden" eines neuen Deutschlands' has been translated into a narrative situation in the post-war part of a novel claiming to examine the genesis of fascism from an unideological, that is, non-fascist perspective.[27] The roots of the novel in all its guises, as well as the essay 'Sexualität und totaler Staat', are, however, relentlessly personal, but, as was suggested above, precisely this disavowal of mass collusion by Austrians in National Socialism made Doderer's novels attractive in the formative years of the Second Republic. Nevertheless, Doderer the historian and Doderer the man had to suffer a bout of creative amnesia to facilitate the work of Doderer the novelist, creator of a comfortably seamless Austro-German identity for the citizens of the Second Republic.

Whereas *Die Dämonen* culminates in the burning of the Palace of Justice in 1927, an event Doderer described as the 'Cannae der österreichischen Freiheit' and which, in his view, triggered the move towards fascism in Austria, *Die Strudlhofstiege*, set in the years 1911–13 and 1923–5, tries to persuade its readers of the essential continuity of Austrian history before and after the First World War which had brought about the end of an ancient Empire. By endlessly stressing personal continuity to the practical exclusion of a calamity as great as the First World War and the collapse of an entire society, Doderer once more highlights the importance of the micro- at the expense of the macro-society. At the same time, by demonstrating that the personal can survive incursions of calamitous historical events, he again makes an important statement for readers of the early 1950s. The message is comforting and consoling: the 'great events' of history are in the end result not those which determine human existence. Like *Die Dämonen*, this earlier novel also shows Jew and Gentile in intimate contact (probably its most attractive character is the Jewish Mary K.) in a Viennese society riddled with personal intrigue but which concludes in a 'happy end': 'um dem lieben Leser die kostbare Erbschaft der Leere, mag sie gleich nur einen idealen Augenblick lang dauern, gleichsam in jungfräulichem Zustande zu hinterlassen.'[28] Doderer's intention that his novel should function as an aid to the restoration of innocence could hardly be more telling.

The final page of *Die Strudlhofstiege* evokes the 'Tiefe der Jahre' in the speech delivered by Amtsrat Julius Zihal, hero of Doderer's previous novel, at the engagement party of the strangely bland 'hero', the erstwhile k.u.k. Major Melzer. The speech attempts a definition of happiness in the context of a forthcoming marriage, but it is also something more, something intended for a 1950s audience in an Austria which, in Doderer's view, had to restore its links with its pre-Nazi past (as defined, of course, by himself): 'denn sie zeigte recht deutlich den Weg, auf dem ein ganzer Volks-Stamm in seiner Eigentümlichkeit allein zum Glücke gelangen, allein sich darin befestigen kann.' Zihal then varies the famous lines from Johann Strauss's *Die Fledermaus*, itself a work written to cheer up a depressed Vienna after the stock market crash of 1874:

> Glücklich ist nicht [. . .] wer vergißt, was nicht mehr zu ändern ist; so etwas kann überhaupt nur in einer Operette vorkommen. Eine derartige Auffassung würde nicht weniger wie ein Unterbleiben der Evidenz bedeuten, beziehungsweise als solches anzusehen sein. Glücklich ist vielmehr derjenige, dessen Bemessung seiner eigenen Ansprüche hinter einem diesfalls herabgelangten höheren Entscheid so weit zurückbleibt, daß dann naturgemäß ein erheblicher Übergenuß eintritt.

The author thus concludes his work with a vision of happiness strongly reminiscent of the Biedermeier, that quiescent period in Austria's history when the middle classes were encouraged to turn away from civic involvement and cultivate their gardens.[29] Doderer's desire to evoke a 'feel-good factor' and to deflect his audience from recent harsh realities is as lively as that of the younger Strauss, hence he creates a work set in the fairly recent, recognizable past but which requires no painful soul-searching on the part of his readership. Thus the events of 1914–18 barely impinge at all, the novel being consciously designed to suggest that the collapse of the Habsburg Empire, but by implication the Third Reich too, has had precious little lasting impact upon the 'real' lives of 'ordinary' people.

Die Strudlhofstiege therefore replicates in epic form the message of the Athens address: that the new Austria should take little account of the most recent past, and that the *Anschluß* which the country should now seek is one with its own, Habsburg-coloured past. The function of the novel is therefore just as much the avoidance of recent history as it is the chronicling of earlier times. It mirrors an attitude which the *émigré* Viennese writer Ernst

Pollack (1909–87) summarized in a poem written at the height of the Waldheim crisis in 1987:

Niemalsland

Wir haben es niemals gewußt.
Wir sind es niemals gewesen.
Das hat es niemals gegeben.

Das ist uns niemals gelungen.
Das haben wir niemals versucht.
Das wurde uns niemals bewiesen.

Protestiert? Das haben wir niemals.
Wir war ja niemals niemals dagegen.
Wir waren auch niemals dafür.

Die Lügen glaubten wir niemals.
Der Ausgang stand niemals in Zweifel.
Denn Frevel lohnt sich doch niemals.

Wir haben niemals gefrevelt.
Wir krümmten niemals ein Haar.
Des hat man uns niemals bezichtigt.

Ja, im Niemalsland lebt sich's behaglich.
Man erinnert sich niemals an nichts.
Uns selber hat's niemals gegeben.

Trotzdem sind wir niemals ganz glücklich.
Wir können halt niemals vergessen
All das, was hier einmal geschah.[30]

Notes

[1] Heimito von Doderer/Albert Paris Gütersloh, *Briefwechsel 1928–1962*, ed. Reinhold Treml (Munich, 1986), p. 38.
[2] Doderer/Gütersloh, *Briefwechsel*, p. 133. See also A. W. Barker, 'Heimito von Doderer and National Socialism', *German Life and Letters*, 41, 2 (1988), 145–58.
[3] H. von Doderer, 'Sexualität und totaler Staat', in W. Schmidt-Dengler

(ed.), *Die Wiederkehr der Drachen. Aufsätze, Traktate, Reden* (Munich, 1970), pp. 275–98. Hereafter this volume will be cited in the body of the text as WdD, with page references after the quotation.

[4] The Athens address was published as 'Le nouveau autrichien', *Cahiers du sud*, 51 (1964), vol. 58, 202–11.

[5] 'Österreichs Nationalbewußtsein ist übernational. Von der Wiederkehr Österreichs', *Die kleine Zeitung* (Graz, 20.6.1964). In *Die Wiederkehr der Drachen* the title 'Athener Rede' is adopted.

[6] Malcolm McInnes, 'Österreich – Österreicher – Am Österreichischten. Heimito von Doderer and Austria', *Colloquia Germanica*, 18 (1985), 18–39. This is all the more significant because two important studies of the mid-1970s had indicated the problematic nature of Doderer's relationship with politics: Anton Reininger, *Die Erlösung des Bürgers: eine ideologiekritische Studie* (Bonn, 1975); Hans Joachim Schroeder, *Apperzeption und Vorurteil. Untersuchungen zur Reflexion Heimito von Doderers* (Heidelberg, 1976).

[7] I am, of course, aware that this overwhelming vote of confidence in Hitler was achieved by the conscious elimination from the vote of the many voices opposed to National Socialism. See Félix Kreissler, 'Semantische Mystifikationen. Vom "Anschluß" über Großdeutschland nach Mitteleuropa und Europa', in Oliver Rathkolb, Georg Schmid and Gernot Heiß (eds.), *Österreich und Deutschlands Größe. Ein schlampiges Verhältnis* (Salzburg, 1990), pp. 15f.

[8] H. von Doderer, *Tangenten. Tagebuch eines Schriftstellers 1940–1950* (Munich, 1964).

[9] See Elizabeth C. Hesson, *Twentieth Century Odyssey: A Study of Heimito von Doderer's 'Die Dämonen'* (Colombia SC, 1982), and Bruce I. Turner, *Doderer and the Politics of Marriage: Personal and Social History in 'Die Dämonen'* (Stuttgart, 1982).

[10] H. von Doderer, *Die Dämonen* (Munich, 1956), pp. 708–806.

[11] E. Brückmüller, *Nation Österreich. Sozialhistorische Aspekte ihrer Entwicklung* (Vienna, 1984), p. 216.

[12] This quotation also appeared in virtually identical form in H. von Doderer, 'Antwort aus Österreich', in Walter von Cube (ed.), *Alpenländische Nachbarschaft* (Munich 1962), p. 100. Quoted in Brückmüller, *Nation Österreich*, p. 217.

[13] Brückmüller, *Nation Österreich*, p. 91.

[14] C. Magris, *Der habsburgische Mythos in der österreichischen Literatur* (Salzburg, 1966).

[15] Brückmüller, *Nation Österreich*, p. 97.

[16] Doderer is a great believer in the benevolence of fate, which will assert itself no matter what in the affairs of man. See, for example, the paradigmatic *Divertimento Nr 5*, written in 1924 but only published for the first time in *Merkur*, 8 (1954), 647–59.

[17] Letter to Gerhard Aichinger, 21 July 1936.

[18] Ibid. See also Gerald Stieg, *Die Frucht des Feuers. Canetti, Doderer, Kraus und der Justizpalastbrand* (Vienna, 1990).

[19] G. Clare, *Last Waltz in Vienna. The Destruction of a Family, 1842–1942* (London, 1982).

[20] See Milan Dubrovic, *Veruntreute Geschichte* (Vienna, 1985), pp. 54f.

[21] M. McInnes, 'Österreich', p. 20.

[22] Dietrich Weber, 'Doderers Wien', *Literatur und Kritik*, 193/194 (April/Mai 1985), 126.

[23] Von Doderer, *Die Dämonen*, p. 309.

[24] D. Weber, 'Doderer's Wien', p. 125.

[25] Quoted from Hesson, *Twentieth Century Odyssey*, p. 23.

[26] Wendelin Schmidt-Dengler, 'Rückzug auf die Sprache', in K. Amann and A. Berger (eds.), *Österreichische Literatur der Dreißiger Jahre* (Vienna, 1985), p. 297.

[27] Hesson, *Twentieth Century Odyssey*, pp. 62f.

[28] H. von Doderer, *Die Strudlhofstiege* (Munich, 1951), p. 908.

[29] Brückmüller is inevitably reminded of the 'Raimund'schen Bescheidenheits-Topoi' (*Nation Österreich*, p. 98).

[30] F. Pollack, 'Niemalsland', in Hannes Krauss (ed.), *Vom Nullpunkt zur Wende. Deutschsprachige Literatur 1945–1960* (Essen, 1994), p. 57.

4

Restoration or Renewal?
Csokor, the Austrian PEN Club and the
Re-establishment of Literary Life in Austria,
1945–1955

MICHAEL MITCHELL

In the introduction to the first volume of his three-volume collection of writers' portraits, *Dichter aus Österreich*, first published in 1956, Norbert Langer wrote of Austrian literature, perhaps intending an implicit contrast with that of the Federal Republic: 'Sie ist stark der Tradition verhaftet, doch ohne eine peinliche Kluft, die durch die schrecklichen Zeitereignisse . . . leicht hätte entstehen können.'[1] If, however, one reads the brief biographies accompanying each of the twenty-five entries, an 'embarrassing gap' very quickly becomes apparent: they contain virtually no dates between 1939 and 1945 (the two exceptions are Werfel's arrival in the USA, 1940, and Ginzkey's move to a house on the Attersee, 1944) and virtually no indication of what the writers did during the Nazi period (Landgrebe and Lernet-Holenia are mentioned as having been in the army, Braun and Wied in exile); there is no mention of contributions to the *Bekenntnisbuch öster-reichischer Dichter* with which the majority of Austrian writers gave enthusiastic welcome to Hitler's annexation of Austria.[2] The article on Weinheber is a good example of the vagueness with which not merely embarrassing facts from, but any connections with, the Hitler period are glossed over or simply ignored: '1932 trat Weinheber in den Ruhestand, um freischaffend seiner Berufung nachkommen zu können. Erfolge, Ehrungen und Preise. In Kirchstetten erwarb er ein eigenes Landhaus, in dem er bis zu seinem Tode arbeitete.'[3] There is not even a mention of the fact that he committed suicide, in case that might prompt the reader to ask why, and perhaps discover the answer – out of remorse and fear of retribution as the Russians approached.

Langer is not alone in his tactful omissions. By the 1950s collective amnesia as to what had happened in the country between 1938 and 1945 was widespread. In Görlich/Romanik's history of Austria, the authors state categorically: 'Der zweite Weltkrieg gehört zur Weltgeschichte, nicht aber zur eigentlich österreichischen Überlieferung. Er war kein österreichischer Krieg. Österreich hat als *Staat* an ihm nicht teilgenommen.'[4] Any responsibility for the war is rejected and with it – implicitly, the question is not even put – any responsibility for the crimes of National Socialism. The authors' excuse for the rapturous welcome given to Hitler borders on the comic:

> Der österreichische Patriot mußte sich sagen, daß nur dir Niederlage Hitlers die Hoffnung auf eine Wiederherstellung des österreichischen Staates in sich berge. Daß dies anfangs hunderttausenden von Österreichern nicht klar war, ist aus den Zeitumständen und der massiven nationalsozialistischen Propaganda her zu erklären.[5]

This, together with the fact that the only sections on the Nazi period are 'Österreichische Opfer' and 'Österreichischer Widerstand', bring it very close to satirical descriptions of the Austrian attitude to the Hitler period such as Robert Neumann's: 'Als Hitler einmarschierte, standen bloß 200 000 Jubelnde am Straßenrand, die Hand erhoben zum Schicklgrubergruß 200 000 sind bloß drei Prozent der Bevölkerung. Demnach gehörten 97 Prozent zum österreichischen Widerstand.'[6] This 'Amnesie als nationale Tugend' was satirized by Hans Georg Behr with two photographs of the scene at the Vienna Heldenplatz in 1938: one 'in historischer Sicht' – the famous picture of crowds cheering Hitler – and one 'in österreichischer Sicht. Nach dem unteren Bild spricht der sogenannte Führer vor einigen zufällig des Weges kommenden Wienern.'[7]

The refusal even to mention fascism as an Austrian problem in Görlich/Romanik's 1970 *Geschichte Österreichs* repeats the attitude, and often the words, expressed in the *Handbuch des Österreichers* published by Görlich in 1949.[8] Although the foreword claims, 'Das österreichische Volk . . . hat das Recht, sich selbst mit allen Vorzügen und Fehlern, mit Licht und Schattenseiten zu sehen', the one 'mistake' or 'dark side' that the book, contrary to this claim, hides from the reader is any connection with fascism. As in the *Geschichte Österreichs*, there are entries under *Widerstandsbewegung* and *Opfer*, but none on *Kollaborateure*; there are articles on *Friedensbewegung* and *Arbeiterbewegung*, but none on political parties, nor on the *Heimwehr*, and certainly not on the NSDAP; on *Kaisertum*, but not on *Republik* or *Ständestaat*; on *österreichische Idee* but not on *Demokratie*.

Görlich's *Handbuch* is an example of the line propagated by conservative sections of Austrian cultural life in the years immediately after 1945, emphasizing continuity with the Empire and 'coming to terms' with the Nazi period by ignoring it or denying that it had anything to do with Austria and Austrians. It was what the publishers of *Das Handbuch des Österreichers* called, in an advertisement in the back of the book, 'die Pflege eines gesunden österreichischen Patriotismus'. However, the significance of the two later works quoted, Langer's *Dichter aus Österreich* and Görlich/Romanik's *Geschichte Österreichs*, lies in the fact that they represent not the views of one section of Austrian life, but what by the early 1950s seems to have become quasi-official policy: both received official support, both were distributed as gifts by the *Unterrichtsministerium* to foreign universities, so that one can assume both represented attitudes to the recent past which officialdom wished to see publicly propagated. Langer's *Dichter aus Österreich* was one of a number of officially sponsored publications, starting around 1951, with the key word *Österreich* in the title. Series such as Stiasny's *Das österreichische Wort* and Bergland's *Österreich-Reihe* were intended largely for home consumption, but will be remembered by many foreign academics from gifts to university libraries. These were all part of what Kurt Bartsch has called 'die offiziöse "austriakische Renaissance", d.h. der von der staatlichen Kulturpolitik subventionierte Versuch, Österreichs Kontinuität durch den Rückgriff auf weit zurückliegende Epochen, gleichsam durch die Wiedergeburt des habsburgischen Erbes zu legitimieren.'[9]

This emphasis on an 'Austrian Idea' associated with the country's cultural history signified the direction cultural policy was to take up to the *Staatsvertrag* and beyond. Until 1950 there had been no consistent line, from either official or unofficial sources, as to the basis on which cultural life in Austria should be rebuilt. Immediately after the war there had been no lack of

voices demanding a complete break with the past and a radical
dissociation from those writers who had compromised with
National Socialism. A good example is the vigorous appeal from
Edwin Rollett, a liberal anti-fascist who had been interned in a
concentration camp under Hitler. He had been active in the
authoritarian *Vaterländische Front* during the 1930s, but after the
war, unlike many others who had been supporters of the *Ständestaat*, was a strong supporter of a democratic renewal based on a
conscious acceptance of the immediate past in Austria. He
wished to see those refugees who had left Austria out of protest
against Hitler encouraged to return to help in this process of
democratic renewal:

> *Wir sind nicht reich genug, gerade unsere Allerbesten in so großer Zahl
> zu entbehren.* Das ist eine Forderung, eine sehr ernste Forderung,
> an alle Seiten und an alle Adressen. Sie richtet sich ganz ebenso
> an alle jene, die Mittel und Kraft dazu haben, unseren Dichtern
> den Weg aus der Emigration nach Österreich und insbesondere
> nach Wien freizumachen . . . Zu einem sind wir aber zweifellos
> und hinreichend reich genug, trotz aller Kargheit. Wir sind reich
> genug, auf alle vom Nationalsozialismus infizierten und ver-
> gifteten ehemaligen Propagandaschreiber und Kollaborateure zu
> verzichten. Wir brauchen sie nicht, wir wollen sie nicht.[10]

Rollett's 'demand' was not met. Relatively few refugees returned
to Austria, and those that did often felt their experiences in emigration shut them off from Austrian cultural life in which all
those 'propagandists and collaborators' were rehabilitated by the
early 1950s.[11]

By 1950, then, the response among cultural leaders to seven
years of Nazi rule was a recourse to a specific Austrian patriotism, which had been conspicuously lacking among the wider
public in the years between the wars. As can be seen from
Görlich/Romanik's implied assertion of the continuance of the
cultural nation after the Austrian state was swallowed up by
the Third Reich, this had the additional advantage of dissocia-
ting Austria and Austrians from the guilt of involvement in
fascism. The adoption of a policy of emphasizing cultural continuity led in the 1950s and early 1960s to a plethora of articles
attempting to define what was particularly Austrian about

Austrian literature, for which the rather worried-sounding sub-title of Herbert Eisenreich's piece might be taken as typical: 'Ist Österreichs Literatur eine österreichische Literatur?'[12] Character-istic also were articles indiscriminately listing any author with a connection with the Habsburg monarchy as a representative of Austrian literature and therefore of some undefined 'Austrian Idea'.[13] This neurotic introspection, in which literary history often degenerated into the repetition of the names of well-known authors as a kind of cultural mantra (to ward off any suggestion of guilty involvement in Nazism?), was parodied by Jörg Mauthe in 1974: 'Heiliger Ferdinand Raimund – bitte für mich. Heiliger Johann Nepomuk von Nestroy – bitte für mich. Heiliger Friedrich von Herzmanovsky – bitte für mich. Ihr drei heiligen Nothelfer der österreichischen Literatur – bittet für mich.'[14]

Edwin Rollett had been pleading for all uncompromised writers to join in 'unsere Arbeit am Bau eines neuen, reinen und klaren Bildes unseres Vaterlandes'. The cultural ideology that emerged from the attempt to build up an Austrian patriotism was certainly not new; as Bartsch suggests in the passage quoted above, it was an ideology which looked back to the Empire, an ideology which was more concerned with establishing continuity than creating its own tradition. There were two concepts that were particularly important in defining Austria's self-image during this period, the *österreichische Idee* and its incarnation in *der österreichische Mensch*. These were presented as the distillation of 'Austrianism' as it had developed down the centuries, as the summation of historical fact, based 'auf nüchterner Feststellung des geschichtlich gewordenen'.[15] They were presented as objec-tive, value-free expressions of the essential Austrian nature, rather than as ideological slogans derived from one specific line of Austrian political development. To quote Görlich again:

> Und doch gelangt man, wenn man die Formulierungen liest, die die österreichische Idee gefunden hat, zur Erkenntinis, daß *der österreichische Gedanke nicht an Staatsformen und Ländergrenzen gebunden ist*, daß er sich im 20. Jahrhundert genau so bewährt hat wie zur Zeit Maria Theresias, in den Tagen des Prinzen Eugen ebenso wie unter Rudolph IV. dem Stifter und den Babenber-gern.[16]

There can be no doubt that a feeling of patriotism and acceptance of one's past is healthy (as Görlich's publishers claimed) for the body politic of a country. But there were dangers concealed in the *Österreich-Ideologie* that was propagated in the 1950s and 1960s. It was not the case, as Görlich asserted, that it was not associated with any particular political structure. In fact, it was the ideology that the *Ständestaat* had tried to propagate in the 1930s, it was Austrian history seen through the prism of Austro-fascism. Its acceptance meant that the Second Republic looked back no further than 1938 for its self-image. This was expressed with rather crude clarity by Alexander Lernet-Holenia: 'In der Tat brauchen wir nur dort fortzusetzen, wo uns die Träume eines Irren [Hitler] unterbrochen haben.'[17] This meant that the *Ständestaat* was interpreted not in its aspect as a semi-fascist Austrian authoritarian state, but solely from the point of view of its opposition to Hitler. Görlich again manages to express this in a manner that is unconsciously satirical. His article in *Das Handbuch des Österreichers* headed 'Widerstandsbewegung' begins:

> Der Widerstand Österreichs gegen den Nationalsozialismus zerfällt in die zwei Perioden von 1933–1938 und 1939–1945. Die Geschichte der ersten Zeit, die durch die Namen Dr. Engelbert Dollfuß (ermordet während der nationalsozialistischen Erhebung am 25. Juli 1934) und Dr. Kurt Schuschnigg gekennzeichnet ist, steht noch heute im Mittelpunkt der Disckussion.[18]

This refusal – or unwillingness – to distinguish between the Third Reich as a state and the ideology behind it allowed those who practised it to present the writers who were representative figures in the *Ständestaat* as model Austrian patriots (and, implicitly, as anti-fascist) to the post-war world. But this begs two important questions. Firstly, it completely ignores the fact that the *Ständestaat* itself was an authoritarian state in which individual liberty and human rights were restricted, and was hardly a suitable model for post-war renewal. Secondly, it ignored the fact that the majority of writers who were representative of the *Ständestaat* were the very writers who allowed themselves to be used by the National Socialists after 1938, in many cases giving the Nazi regime enthusiastic support.[19] Their appearance as pillars of official cultural policy in the 1950s meant that the atmosphere was not conducive to any meaningful process of denazification. These Austrian 'cultural collaborators' were often justified by the myth that any artistic activity that was not specifically pro-Nazi was an act of inner resistance. The conservative Catholic periodical, *Die Furche*, was peddling this theory as early as 1946:

> Nicht wenige führende Männer des Geistes und der Kultur haben durch ihr Ausharren in der Heimat unersetzliche Kulturwerte vor Unkultur und Verrohung bewahrt, indem sie irgendwie mit den widerlich-trostlosen Zeitumständen in Klugheit oder List fertig zu werden suchten.[20]

This sentence deserves detailed stylistic analysis (for example, what a world of prevarication is contained in *irgendwie*!), but the point relevant to the current argument is that the phrase 'Ausharren in der Heimat', besides dignifying what was often crude opportunism, contains an implicit condemnation of the refugees, who could be seen as having deserted the *Vaterland*.[21] The article does, of course, also contain an acknowledgement of the work of Austrian refugees; but the tone is patronizing and almost offhand in comparison with the praise of those who 'stood by their country': 'Gewiß, es soll nicht vergessen werden, daß viele gute Österreicher während der schweren Jahre im Ausland sich unablässig und kraftvoll zu ihrem Vaterland – Österreich – bekannt haben.'[22] And it does not praise the refugees for their anti-fascist or democratic stance, but simply for support of the 'Austria' that was to become the focus of establishment cultural policy in the 1950s. There is no suggestion, for example, that returning refugees might have something to offer cultural life in the new Austria from their experiences in countries not submerged in fascism, or from having worked together with various anti-fascist groups.

Thus the atmosphere in Austrian cultural life was not welcoming to those in exile whom Rollett had hoped it would be government policy to try to entice back, and the public in general had no ear for the themes deriving from the exile experiences they wished to write about. The onset of the Cold War, of course, was an important added factor in creating a cultural and political situation which was much more favourable to conservative elements who had remained in the country under Hitler than to

returning exiles. That cultural life in the 1950s was determined
largely by those who had 'stood by their country', rather than by
those who had spent the time 'abroad', can be seen in the names
of those awarded the literary prizes. Klaus Amann gives a list of
twenty-five prominent Austrian authors alive at the time who
did not belong to the group of 'die betont vaterländischen und
nationalen Autoren', and notes 'Nennenswerte Auszeichnungen
erhielten von allen diesen Autoren im Jahrzehnt 1950–1960
lediglich Csokor (Staatspreis 1955, Preis der Stadt Wien 1953),
Bruckner (Preis der Stadt Wien 1957), und Kramer (Preis der
Stadt Wien 1958).'[23]

An acknowledgement of fascism as an Austrian problem and
an examination of its manifestations both in the home-grown
Ständestaat and in the imposed National Socialist *Ostmark* had to
wait until the late 1970s. How long this unwillingness to face up
to Austrians' involvement in fascism lasted can be seen in the
fate of the two novels of the 1960s which dealt with it. Hans
Lebert's *Die Wolfshaut* (1960), and Gerhard Fritsch's *Fasching*
(1967) were largely ignored; it is only recently that Lebert's novel
has been reissued, Fritsch's is still out of print.[24] An example of
the mental distance Austrian academics had to travel can be seen
in the work of Viktor Suchy. In 1959 he wrote the introduction to
the fiftieth volume of Stiasny's patriotic series, *Das österreichische
Wort*, an anthology with the same title as the series.[25] His introduction is an uncritical regurgitation of the 'Austrian' ideology
(often quoting the extreme nationalist literary historian, Josef
Nadler), proclaiming it as the appropriate culture for post-war
Austria: 'Diese Worte [Hofmannsthal on the 'Austrian Idea']
erhalten ihre wahre Bedeutung erst nach 1945!'[26] There is in this
introduction not the least hint of his insight of 1977 that the
'Austrian Idea', whatever its inherent truth as a reflection of
Austrian history, was unsuitable as a guide for cultural life after
1945 because it had been misused by the semi-fascist *Ständestaat*:

> Nun 'gefunden' wurde diese Idee noch während des ersten
> Weltkriegs, als die Doppelmonarchie ihren Todeskampf ausfocht.
> Konserviert und im Kampf gegen den Anschlußgedanken der
> Deutschnationalen . . . sowie gegen die heraufziehende Barbarei
> des Nationalsozialismus als ideologisches Abwehrmittel wurde
> diese Idee dann in der Ersten Republik und im autoritären

Ständestaat eingesetzt, der den faschistischen Teufel mit dem kleriko-faschistoiden Beelzebub austreiben wollte.[27]

The question that naturally arises is why an opposition to the literary establishment did not arise in Austria as it very quickly did in West Germany. The standard picture of literary life in Austria up to the 1960s is the one painted by Walter Weiß: 'Bis weit in die fünfziger Jahre hinein bot das literarische Leben in Österreich das Bild eines nicht grundsätzlich gestörten Neben- und Miteinanders verschiedener Schriftstellergenerationen.'[28] Traditionalists of the older generation and youthful avant-gardists co-operated, the former often fostering the latter. More sur- prising, perhaps, is the lack of any group involved in *political* opposition to the establishment. Weiss's explanation is that of the major figures of the preceding generation only a few were 'com- promised'. This is being very selective: the examples he gives of that generation are Musil, Broch, Roth, Werfel, Zweig, Canetti, Gütersloh, Doderer. This is what that generation looks like from *today's* perspective, but Musil, Broch and so on were dead or in exile and were not the names a young writer in Vienna in the late 1940s would have thought of when asking how far the older gen- eration was compromised by association with National Socialism. The explanation for the lack of any strong impulse towards an *Abrechnung* with the older generation *à la Gruppe 47* is more likely to reside in Austria's confused and confusing situa- tion as a cross between defeated enemy and liberated victim, which blurred the distinction between Nazi and non-Nazi. The confusion was added to by the adoption of the Austrian ideology of the *Ständestaat* which, as we have seen, had been most strongly promoted by those who had proved to be most susceptible to the attractions of the Nazi invaders. Also, the existence of an alterna- tive German-language literature meant that writers who might have formed an anti-establishment group in Austria could emi- grate to the Federal Republic. Perhaps the existence of *Gruppe 47* in the Federal Republic rendered an Austrian equivalent super- fluous. This would be a parallel to the 1920s and early 1930s, when radical Austrian dramatists such as Csokor, Ferdinand Bruckner and Ödön von Horvath had their greatest triumphs in Weimar Germany.

The initial unity between the generations under the flag of the

'Austrian Idea' can be seen in the career of Gerhard Fritsch. He was a member of the younger generation (born in 1924) who rapidly became an important figure on the literary scene, editor of important anthologies and of magazines such as *Wort in der Zeit* and *Literatur und Kritik*. His first novel, *Moos auf den Steinen* (1956), conformed to the prevailing outlook by examining in fairly positive terms the relevance of Austria's cultural heritage for the present. His second novel, *Fasching*, is both experimental in style and a slashing attack on Austrian fascism in content. Despite his position as one of the central figures in the Austrian literary scene, the novel was ignored, did not sell, and was not reprinted. Even when an anti-establishment faction appeared in Austria, its opposition was artistic rather than political. Austria had to wait until the late 1970s and 1980s for the kind of research which revealed the connections between the *Ständestaat*, the Nazis, and continuing fascist attitudes.

The shining exception in Langer's gallery of glossed-over portraits is Franz Theodor Csokor. He is the one writer in the collection whose activities during the Hitler period are adequately recorded. Csokor, who was one of the relatively small number of refugees who returned to Austria soon after the war, had gone into voluntary exile on 18 March 1938, and spent the war years in Poland, Romania, Yugoslavia and Italy, where he worked for the Allies' psychological warfare department, producing newspapers and radio programmes directed at Austria. Within the confines of a brief biographical note, all this is given due weight by Langer:

> Als Mitglied des internationalen PEN-Clubs protestierte er 1933 auf dem Kongress in Dubrovnik gegen die Unterdrückung der Freiheit des Denkens und Schaffens, gegen die Methoden des Dritten Reichs. Im Zeichen des Protestes verließ er 1938 Wien, obwohl ihn hiezu kein rassischer Grund nötigte. Er ging über Warschau nach Rumänien, von dort nach Jugoslawien und Italien. Im Dienste der Alliierten kam er 1944 nach Rom, wo er bis Kriegsende bei den Sendungen des BBC für Österreich wirkte.[29]

Even here, Langer's formulation gives one pause for thought. The words fascism or National Socialism do not appear. Csokor's opposition is merely to the 'methods' of Hitler's Germany; his work for the Allies is not described as 'anti-fascist propaganda' but as 'für Österreich', thus fitting him into the conservative tradition of Austrian patriotism discussed above, rather than into the tradition of European liberal humanism, to which he properly belongs.

Csokor's name was, of course, also associated with the idea of an Austrian patriotism going back to the old monarchy through his play *Dritter November 1918*. His own description of it as 'eine Art Requiem des letzten Restes des Heiligen Römischen Reiches, das wir bis 1918 waren'[30] appears to place it firmly in the tradition of the 'Austrian Idea' that goes back through Maria Theresa and Prinz Eugen to the Babenbergers. The fact that the play is an attempt to deal with the rise of extreme nationalism in the 1930s through the portrayal of the humane, multinational society that the old Empire symbolized for Csokor was, and still is, generally ignored.[31] But the fact remained that within the context of Austrian cultural politics in the early post-war years, Csokor was seen as having a foot in both camps. His situation is well described in the recollections of Paul Blaha:

> Der unerschütterliche Weltverbesserer, der Mann zwischen Büchner, Trakl und Horváth, der Emigrant, der gewissermaßen Emigrant blieb, auch in Wien, als er zurückgekommen war, verkörperte die Monarchie *und* die Revolution, den Vielvölkerstaat *und* dessen Zusammenbruch, die romantische Vorkriegs-Bohème *und* ihre katastrophale Existenz in der Zwischenkriegszeit, die Depression *und* den Antifaschismus.[32]

With such credentials, it is hardly surprising that Csokor was seen as the ideal figure to head the Austrian PEN (Poets, Playwrights, Editors, Essayists and Novelists) Club, when it was re-established in Vienna. He returned to Vienna in 1946, as a member of the occupying forces, but had to rejoin his unit in Italy, before finally settling in Vienna in 1947. He had been a member of the pre-war PEN, and during his visit in 1946 he was involved in discussions about the return of the exiled Austrian PEN centre in London to Vienna. At the PEN Congress in Zurich in 1947, which accepted the re-establishment of an Austrian PEN centre, it was Csokor, together with Alexander Sacher-Masoch, who had shared his exile in Yugoslavia, who represented the Austrian side. And it was Csokor, both in the speech he made and in his person, who convinced the other nations represented in the PEN Club of the anti-fascist ethos of the proposed Austrian PEN.

The presidency of the PEN Club gave Csokor an influential role in literary Vienna, but it also placed him in one of the more exposed positions of post-war Austrian cultural life. Although not the only writers' association, it was the only one which was required by an outside body – the PEN International – to pursue a denazification policy. Csokor soon found himself in the cross-fire between the left and right wings, which intensified with the onset of the Cold War. But the political side was only one aspect of the work of the re-established PEN Club, if the most publicized. It continued the tradition of practical help to writers in difficulties begun by Robert Neumann in the exiled centre in London, and provided both financial and organizational support to a large number of writers. As well as this, in the first decade of the new republic, the PEN Club was generally recognized by the government as the representative writers' organization and frequently consulted as such. During the years prior to the *Staatsvertrag* the PEN Club's status as part of an international organization made it important to a government that was concerned to re-establish its status as a fully independent state. In particular, the Austrians welcomed anything that differentiated them from the Germans, and the re-establishment of the Vienna PEN centre in 1947, one year before the Germans were allowed back, was celebrated by Csokor and Sacher-Masoch as 'einer der ersten – wenn nicht überhaupt *der* erste – außenpolitische Erfolg unseres Landes seit Kriegsende', in which they were supported by the minister for education, Felix Hurdes.[33] For similar reasons, the holding of the annual PEN Congress in Vienna in 1955 was regarded as evidence of Austria's regained status in the cultural world and enthusiastically supported by the government. It was to be both the high point and the culmination point of the PEN Club's leading role in Austrian literary life. New groupings, especially representing younger authors, then took the creative initiative, leaving what was regarded as the old-fashioned PEN Club its representative function – which, interestingly enough, is more or less where it started out.

The PEN Club had been founded in England in 1921, as a response to the First World War, 'to promote tolerance and friendliness'.[34] It quickly became an international organization, with a distinguished membership, but to begin with it was, in spite of its high-minded origins, 'little more than a dining club which met monthly and often entertained foreign writers'.[35] Internationalist and humanitarian in its origins, the club remained resolutely non-political, a position emphatically endorsed by its first president, John Galsworthy, who stated categorically, 'No politics in the PEN Club under any circumstances'.[36] This stance fitted in well with the general atmosphere of international co-operation in the 1920s,[37] but came under increasing pressure in the thirties and led to heated debates at PEN Congresses between those who wished to remain non-political at all costs and those, like H. G. Wells, who insisted that there were cases where the club's principles of humanity and toleration necessitated taking sides. In several cases in the later thirties the Club managed to have its cake and eat it by establishing appeal funds for Catalan, Austrian and Czech writers forced to leave their countries, while rejecting motions condemning the governments that had driven them into exile.

Initially, the history of the Austrian PEN paralleled that of its parent body, but in the thirties, because of its close links with Germany, and because of Austrian writers' dependence on the German market, it became much more deeply involved in cultural politics. According to its historian, Klaus Amann:

> Das wichtigste Forum für diese Auseinandersetzung [between right-wing nationalist and liberal authors] wurde in Österreich der P.E.N.-Club, der sich damit unversehens von einer literarischen Nachmittagsgesellschaft in eine politische Arena verwandelt sah, in der sich – sichtbar für alle Interessierten – die Spaltung der österreichischen Schriftsteller in Nutznießer und Verfolgte des Dritten Reiches vollzog.[38]

The parting of the ways came at the 1933 PEN congress in Dubrovnik where a resolution condemning the book-burnings in Germany was agreed. The official Austrian delegates, Felix Salten and Grete Urbanitzky, either remained silent (Salten), or joined the German delegates in walking out (Urbanitzky). Csokor and others attending the Congress stayed to support the resolution, with the result that their works were immediately banned in Germany. This was followed up by a general meeting of the

Austrian PEN in Vienna at which a resolution was accepted condemning the restrictions on writers' freedom in Germany which
led to the resignation of extreme nationalist authors, followed by
a number of conservative Catholic writers. But this was quickly
followed by a political swing in the other direction when in 1934,
following the emigration of a number of liberal and left-wing
members, the Vienna centre was taken over by conservatives loyal
to the authoritarian *Ständestaat*.

The Austrian PEN Club was liquidated after the *Anschluß*, but
lived on in the London centre, set up and managed throughout
the war by one of the *émigrés* of 1934, Robert Neumann. By the
time it returned to Vienna in 1947, the international PEN had
abandoned its non-political stance to the extent of including anti-
fascism in its humanitarian principles. For this reason, the re-
established Austrian PEN looked back not to the club as it existed
in 1938, but to the liberal body that had existed briefly between
the Dubrovnik congress and the conservative take-over in 1934.
That is, those who set up the Vienna PEN centre saw it as establishing continuity with a *different* tradition from the one that
gradually emerged as quasi-official cultural policy between 1950
and 1955.

In line with the international PEN Club's stance in the years
immediately after 1945, the anti-fascist credentials of new members and of those applying for readmission were checked. This
imposition often irritated the Austrians, seeming to them to be
outside interference in what should be an independent organization. They were, of course, particularly susceptible to this kind of
irritation precisely because the country did not enjoy full independence. Even Csokor complained that outsiders, for example
writers who had not returned from exile, did not understand the
complexities of the situation in Vienna. For example, Jews who
had suffered in concentration camps sometimes made pleas for
writers who had supported Hitler, and writers who had collab-
orated with the Nazis in public had often assisted socialist or
Jewish colleagues in private. Csokor gave the example of the
most notorious Nazi among Austrian authors, Mirko Jelusisch,
who, in 1938, had still publicly embraced Csokor, even after
he had told him of his intention to leave Austria, and who, as
director of the Burgtheater, assisted Jewish members of the
ensemble to emigrate.[39] A further complicating factor was the

attitude of the Allies, especially the Americans, as Csokor indicated in a reply to Ludwig Ullmann's complaint from the USA in
1948 that people compromised by their behaviour under the
Nazis were reappearing in Austrian literary life: 'Gegen diese
Dinge – die von der Gegend, in der du wohnst, protegiert werden
– anzukämpfen, fällt hier allerdings nicht leicht.'[40]

There was also inconsistency in the decisions reached. Nabl
and Mell, for example, were quickly readmitted, in spite of their
close co-operation with the Nazi regime; Doderer, who had been
a member of the Nazi Party before 1938, but had rejected National
Socialism by 1940, was refused admission when he applied in
1947, and had to wait until 1952; Arnolt Bronnen, another former
member of the Nazi Party, was also rejected, even in 1952, but in
his case the cause of his rejection is less likely to have been his
Nazi past than his Communist present.

Ultimately very little was done to keep the PEN Club free of
writers who were compromised by their collaboration with fascism. Between 1948 and 1952, there were sixteen cases of authors
being barred, and many of those were successful with a subsequent application. In this the PEN Club's efforts reflected what
was happening on the governmental level: a *Literaturreinigungs-
gesetz* was passed by the Parliament, but never came into force; a
'list of banned authors' established by the Education Ministry
contained, in 1948, only six names.[41] Despite the conditions set
by PEN International, despite pressure from Austrians who had
remained in exile, and despite the impeccable personal anti-fascist record of several of its leading committee members such as
Csokor, Sacher-Masoch and Edwin Rollett, the Austrian PEN Club
found it impossible to swim against the tide of public feeling and
official attitudes, especially given the numerical superiority in
Vienna of writers who had 'stood by their country' under Hitler
over those who had gone into exile.

Besides the attempted denazification, there were two other
aspects of the PEN programme which were more in the nature of
positive action, and reflected Csokor's own concerns. In the first
place, he and Alexander Sacher-Masoch organized readings of
Austrian writers who had gone into exile or been murdered in
the concentration camps, and other commemorative meetings for
those who had died or been killed. Authors thus celebrated
included, for example, Franz Werfel, Ferdinand Bruckner, Stefan

Zweig, Robert Musil, Hermann Broch, Jura Soyfer, Karl Roman Scholz and Felix Grafe. This was part of an attempt in the immediate post-war years to awaken awareness of an anti-fascist and democratic vein in Austrian literature as the foundation for literary life in 'liberated' Austria. Together with other efforts in this direction, of which Otto Basil's magazine *Plan* is the best-known, this was to founder on the twin rocks of public lack of interest and the emergence of the conservative 'Austrian Idea' as the basis for establishment cultural policy.

Csokor also hoped that the newly reconstituted PEN Club might have a role to play in the international field. His plan was that the Austrian centre should try to foster particularly close relations with its immediate neighbours who had been part of the old Habsburg Empire. This was not at all the cultural imperialism to which the 'Austrian' ideology occasionally sailed dangerously close. It stemmed from his true internationalism of outlook and from his experiences during exile. It was also connected with his involvement in the peace movement during the later 1940s. His initiatives in this direction, which began at the congress at which the Austrian PEN Club was re-established, were very quickly swallowed up in the tide of propaganda that was released by the Cold War. Fifteen years later, in the mid-1960s, the development of cultural ties with the Communist states of Eastern Europe became a feature of Austrian foreign policy, something which gave him great satisfaction.[42] In this area of policy, Csokor's influence stretched well beyond 1955 or 1965, and even beyond his death. His ideal of a real cultural dialogue with the nations of Eastern Europe was brought to fruition, both within the PEN Club and in a wider context, by a Hungarian *émigré* who was also to become president of the PEN Club, György Sebestyén, to whom Csokor had given encouragement and support when he fled to Vienna in 1956.

By the end of the 1940s, however, the international climate had changed from co-operation to confrontation, and the onset of the Cold War became one of the most important factors influencing cultural life in Austria. In that context, anti-fascism, especially in co-operation with left-wing groups, which had been a common war experience of the exiled writers, was seen as crypto-communism. An example of how soon the equation 'anti-fascism = communism' became established can be seen in the comments on

Niemals vergessen, a 1946 exhibition on National Socialism, in the autobiography of Rudolf Henz, a director of Austrian radio in the *Ständestaat*, and one of the leading proponents of the 'back-to-1938' line: 'Hinter der Parole "Niemals vergessen" stand bereits kaum sichtbar die Aufforderung: "Hinein in die Volksdemokratie!"'[43]

If some of the discussions regarding denazification were acrimonious, they were largely held within the confines of the club and did not receive wide publicity. Exceptions, such as the cases of the academic writers, Josef Nadler and Heinz Kindermann, only serve to prove the rule.[44] The argument arising from the Cold War, however, was much more public and much more vitriolic.

It was understandable that feelings in Austria should run high on this subject. Many people there felt exposed as, one after the other, the Eastern European democracies became Soviet satellites – Poland in 1947, Czechoslovakia in 1948 and Hungary in 1949 – leaving occupied Austria very much in the front line. The Communist tactic of using 'bloc politics', of joining a 'popular front' or a 'democratic bloc' as a covert means of extending their own control rendered *any* organization collaborating with Communists – or, eventually, not specifically opposed to them – open to accusations of being crypto-communist. Even Robert Neumann, a left-winger who in the immediate post-war years had attempted to establish a PEN centre in the Soviet Union, changed his tune. By 1950 he was warning Vienna (he had stayed in England) against Communist influence, and even recommended to them the virtues of *Proporz*, suggesting that their PEN committee might be reorganized to reflect the political composition of the government. That this was the very person who only three years earlier had insisted that the first condition for re-establishing a Vienna PEN centre was that it should be completely independent of both the Austrian government and the Allied administration shows how deeply Cold-War attitudes had penetrated. Organizations such as the PEN Club, which tried to maintain a dialogue with the new 'peoples' democracies', which, as has been mentioned above, was part of Csokor's programme, were suspected of letting themselves be used, wittingly or unwittingly, as Trojan horses bearing communist influence. Arguing within the context of a much used image of the time, Csokor insisted that he wanted the society to remain a 'bridge'; his opponents attacked it as a 'bridgehead' for communist influence.

The Cold-War debate was conducted in fairly robust terms, and Csokor was subjected to frequent personal abuse in the press. In a short essay looking back on the years after 1945, Friedrich Heer recalled this depressing aspect of Austrian literary life:

> Ich wurde, ohne besondere Bemühung meinerseits, Mitglied des PEN-Clubs, nahm kaum je an einer Sitzung teil, weil mir die Animositäten nicht lagen und besonders nicht der Kampf gegen den tapferen Csokor, der von Leuten, deren Namen ich heute nicht nennen möchte, pausenlos als idiotischer Fellow-Traveller der 'Bolschewiken' angegriffen wurde.[45]

The chief of those whom Heer preferred not to name was Hans Weigel (the other was Friedrich Torberg), who again and again returned to the subject of communist influence in the executive of the Austrian PEN Club, which had, he claimed, 'das Recht verwirkt, als repräsentativ für das österreichische Geistesleben zu gelten'.[46] Weigel even unearthed a play full of patriotic sentiment Csokor had written almost forty years earlier, on the outbreak of the First World War, in order to try to discredit him.[47]

Csokor and the majority of the PEN committee resisted these attempts to absorb the Club into the system of *Proporz*, refusing, for example, to accept the resignation of the last communist among them, Ernst Fischer. Although they had largely been forced to succumb to the prevailing wind as far as denazification was concerned, they did succeed in retaining a modicum of independence in the Cold-War atmosphere, remaining the one place where a degree of peaceful coexistence was still practised. Csokor responded to these attacks with the same dignity with which he had borne similar abuse during the denazification debates. In his comments on Weigel's defence at a trial in 1955, Csokor reasserted his commitment to the PEN Club's principles of 'tolerance and friendliness', despite the fact that a public commitment to 'peace' was still at the time generally regarded as a cypher for communist influence: 'In meinem ganzen Leben war ich nie Mitglied einer politischen Partei! Hingegen bekenne ich mich als Präsident des österreichischen Penclubzentrum mit seiner Forderung nach Toleranz, Humanität und Freiheit des Schaffens zu einer in Frieden lebenden Menschheit.'[48]

Csokor's personal honesty and his reputation as a man who

had refused to compromise his beliefs in 1938 marked him out as a natural person to play a leading role in the re-establishment of literary life in Austria after the end of the war. When he returned to Vienna, he must surely also have expected to play at least as important a role through his literary works, in particular his plays. And this was, initially, the case. A play he brought back with him from exile, *Kalypso*, was the first by a living Austrian author to be mounted by the Burgtheater ensemble in 1946, and was taken to Switzerland on their first foreign tour in that year. The review of *Kalypso* in the *Arbeiterzeitung* called Csokor 'gegenwärtig Wiens bedeutendster Dramatiker'; Jethro Bithell wrote in 1954, 'It is more or less a *cliché* that as a dramatist he counts as equal with Zuckmayer and Bert Brecht';[49] for Norbert Langer, 'Csokor gehört zusammen mit Ferdinand Bruckner und Fritz Hochwälder zu den repräsentativen österreichischen Dramatikern der Gegenwart.'[50]

However, in spite of his initial assumption of the role of *the* contemporary Austrian dramatist, his ambitions in that respect were not to be fulfilled. He never repeated the success of his plays of the late twenties and thirties such as *Gesellschaft der Menschenrechte, Besetztes Gebiet* or *Dritter November 1918*. In the first few years his plays did reach the stage, but achieved nothing more than *succès d'estime*, and were taken off after a relatively small number of performances.[51] *Die Zeit*, in 1950, expressed surprise at his eclipse:

> Sind wirklich außer Brecht und Zuckmayer keine Dramatiker da, die in deutscher Sprache Stücke für ein lebendiges und gegenwärtiges Theater schreiben? Die Dramaturgen behaupten es. Aber man wird an ihrer Skepsis irre, wenn man Bekanntschaft mit Franz Theodor Csokors *Gottes General* macht und sich verwundert fragt, warum die großen Bühnen an dem Werk des Wiener Autors vorübergehen.[52]

Bithell, in his 1954 article, asks the same question: 'today he is off the stage, and strangely enough in Austria as well as in Germany. The problem for the critic then is: why is a dramatist whose plays palpitate with contemporary interest so neglected?'[53]

One reason for Csokor's lack of success was a widespread indifference both among the Viennese public and in the theatre world itself precisely to plays that 'palpitated with contemporary interest'. His *littérature engagée* fell foul of 'one of the most fatal traits of the Austrian character: the tendency to look the other way whenever unpleasant facts have to be faced'.[54] Audiences and theatres looked back to the past, either to avoid having to face up to the present, or as part of the ideology of the 'Austrian Idea':

> Die Spielpläne erfüllten in hohem Maß die Erwartungen der um Ruhe und Ordnung und geistigen Wiederaufbau Besorgten. Sie werden von Klassikern und von Unterhaltungsware, die oft in die Zeit der Monarchie zurückführt, in die goldene, alte Zeit, dominiert. Die Werke der Zwischenkriegszeit mit ihrem Engagement, ihrem Mut zu neuer Sicht alter Probleme, mit dem Versuch, die traditionellen Mauern niederzureißen, werden ängstlich umgangen . . . Aber auch der Gegenwart und der unmittelbaren Vergangenheit stellt man sich nur mit Vorbehalten.[55]

The one play of Csokor's that was given several productions was, of course, *Dritter November 1918*,[56] the one which could most easily be fitted into the wave of nostalgia and the prevailing 'Austrian' ideology. But *Kalypso* and *Der verlorene Sohn* were the kind of *Emigrantenliteratur* for which there was no audience in Vienna, whilst *Caesars Witwe* foundered, at least in part, on the very urbanity with which it dealt with the theme of totalitarianism versus the rights of the individual.

Besides these relative failures, which is what *succès d'estime* really denotes, there were the plays which did not even reach the stage. Several of these had precisely the *engagement* that Greisenegger, quoted above, sees as lacking in the post-war Austrian theatre. *Gottes General* (performed in Hamburg in 1950) is a portrait of a spiritual hero, St Ignatius, which Csokor originally conceived as an antidote to the heroic men of action so beloved of fascism. In *Pilatus* (written 1948–9), Palestine is an occupied country, like the Yugoslavia where Csokor had spent much of the war. Barabbas and Christ represent two opposing aspects of resistance: Barabbas and his followers believe in armed conflict in the national cause, Christ seeks to transform the lives of his opponents, an approach also formulated by His servant, Ignatius, 'Ich gehe mit jedem durch seine Türe hinein, um ihn durch meine Türe hinauszuführen'.[57]

A much more radical departure, both in theme and structure, is *Wenn sie zurückkommen*, written, as was *Kalypso*, during his exile on the island of Korcula. In twelve scenes, two-handers and monologues forming a kind of inverted, post-coital *Reigen* for women, it shows women who have just returned from making love. In focusing on women alone, it gives their experiences an independence, an equal weight with those of men, which anticipates, in this if not in the precise analysis of women's situation, more recent feminist literature. However, in theme as well as in origin it belongs to Csokor's exile writings. His experiences, particularly with the partisans, convinced him that after the war women would not want to return quietly to their previous dependence (another play of this period, *Medea postbellica*, explores this theme of the problems of a female partisan returning to a peace-time existence). *Wenn sie zurückkommen* was performed in a small theatre in Vienna in 1947, but was too far ahead of its time. Its attempt to 'tear down traditional barriers' in both theme and form was precisely what the Viennese theatre and its public did not want.

A brief examination of his three plays that were premiered by the Burgtheater ensemble between 1945 and 1955 – *Kalypso*, *Der verlorene Sohn* and *Caesars Witwe* – will illustrate further the reasons for his lack of success in the theatre. *Kalypso* uses the Odysseus legend, a very common topos of exile literature. But what made this play the kind of *Emigrantenliteratur* to which the Viennese public could not, or would not, relate was not simply the choice of the Odysseus topos, but the way Csokor characterizes his hero. Odysseus is not the exile driven by longing to return home (which would have allowed the audience to equate Vienna with a longed-for Ithaca), but the incarnation of male restlessness. He cannot settle anywhere, cannot accept the peace Kalypso and Penelope offer. This restlessness continually draws him into conflicts, which he sees as the *raison d'être* of his life. Otto Koenig, a fellow member of the PEN committee, noted in his perceptive *Arbeiterzeitung* review of the first performance that Odysseus is 'seiner natürlichen Heimat entfremdet'. The rather pessimistic conclusion to the play is that war will continue until men change. The audience was probably further estranged by allusions to the recently ended war in, for example, the iron-clad Stymphalian birds, recalling the aircraft that had been flying over

Vienna only a year before, and by a deliberate mixture of theatrical styles ranging from the high pathos of *der blinde Sänger* (Homer), to the chitter-chatter of the empty-headed society goddess, Galathea, who comes from the burlesqued world of Giraudoux's *Amphitryon 38*.

Der verlorene Sohn is set in the Yugoslavia torn between the occupying German forces and the partisans that Csokor knew from his own years of exile. In this play, too, Csokor refused to provide his audience with a comforting message, for example that after the horrors of war the world was back in joint again. The play focuses on the father whose youngest, and favourite, son Stipe, the 'prodigal son' of the title, has joined the partisans. The father, Otac, is forced into a tragic situation where he must sacrifice either Stipe or his two elder sons. Whatever solution he comes to (he sacrifices the two eldest to his 'prodigal son') means that the play cannot have a positive ending. The liberation is as bloody as the occupation, the partisans are seen as having sacrificed their individual humanity to a cause as much as the occupying Germans, even though it may be to a better cause. The future perspective is, as in *Kalypso*, one of continuing conflict, in this case one in which 'Es geht auch nicht um Grenzen oder Völker . . . Es geht um arm und reich, um Knecht und Herr'.[58] It was not a message that the audience of 1947 wanted to hear, and by 1950 it was one which would, for many, put the author in suspicion of being on the wrong side of the Cold War.

Kalypso and *Der verlorene Sohn* were plays Csokor had written in exile and brought back with him to Vienna, and both foundered not only on the public's indifference to the wider experience of writers returning from exile, but also on the Burgtheater's own lack of commitment: 'Diesmal jedoch [in *Der verlorene Sohn*], wo der eminente Dramatiker Csokor zu spüren ist, versagt das Burgtheater und liefert eine Realisierung zweiter, ja dritter Wahl – was in Zukunft immer wieder ein Merkmal der "Pflege" von Werken österreichischer Zeitgenossen sein soll.'[59] After *Der verlorene Sohn* in 1947, the man who was regularly referred to as 'one of Austria's leading dramatists' had to wait until 1955 for a major Viennese production of a new play.

This play was *Caesars Witwe*, written in the early fifties and put on at the Akademietheater in 1955 in celebration of Csokor's seventieth birthday. It consists of an argument, drawn out over four decades, between Caesar's widow, Calpurnia, and Caesar's heir, Augustus. Csokor uses this confrontation to discuss the question of totalitarianism versus individual freedom. Augustus, after twenty years of the *pax romana*, which we still associate with his name, can argue persuasively that the killing of 'two thousand politicians' is justified by the twenty years of peace that have followed. Calpurnia feels instinctively that there is a flaw in the argument, but, limited by the attitudes of the age in which she lives, cannot put her finger on it. The answer does not come until she is on her death-bed when, in an adumbration of the birth of Christ, she has a sudden insight that faith and the individual are more important than rational calculation and the masses. This urbane and amusing dissection of the use and abuse of political power was a further *succès d'estime* for the Grand Old Man of the Austrian theatre, but did not provoke any real debate, and was not the kind of play other theatres felt they had to put on.

This result is despite the fact that the underlying theme had great contemporary resonance, being applicable to the Soviet states of Eastern Europe as well as to the Nazi past (another factor which allowed Austrians to ignore the personal relevance and view their own recent past as part of an anti-communist movement and therefore, seen from the vantage point of the Cold War, basically justified). The pompous and empty *Friedensfeier* that Augustus organizes as part of the self-glorification that helps to cement his power has echoes of the peace organizations that were generally regarded in the West as Trojan horses for communist influence.[60] On the other hand, the order that everyone should hang palm branches from their windows as part of a 'vom Princeps Augustus geforderte freie Willenskundgebung unseres Volkes' and the cries of 'Prin-ceps! Prin-ceps!'[61] have clear echoes of the National Socialist state.

Through the figure of Augustus, Csokor is attacking the general question of totalitarianism, as, for example, in Ausgustus' use of fear to establish his control, and in his claim that it is done for the sake of the people. But he also establishes links with Austria for those willing to listen. Maeson, the emperor's Greek secretary, describes Augustus' greatest achievement as the creation of 'Der römische Mensch'.[62] This is a clear reference to 'der öster-reichische Mensch' which was a keystone of the 'Austrian' ideology propagated by the *Ständestaat* which had become quasi-official cultural policy by the time the play was performed. The retort of the young hothead, Sextus, – 'Dein römischer Mensch ist ein Feigling geworden, ein Herdenvieh, das sein "Ja" blökt zu allem, was dein Princeps verlangt' – is confirmed by the fact that Calpurnia is the only person left in Rome with the strength to stand up to Augustus. In her final confrontation with him she realizes that 'der römische Mensch' is less than a plain 'Mensch', not more. The ideal she now perceives is focused on the individual, which is central to Csokor's own outlook: 'Wie er [Julius Caesar] uns Gesetze und Zeit zu erneuern verstand, so suchte er auch eine weisere Ordnung, die nicht bloß die Menschen unserer Provinzen in Römer verwandelt hätte, sondern unsere Römer zu Menschen im Reich seines Planes.'[63]

The prime example of the way Romans have spinelessly submitted to Augustus is his poet laureate, Horace. He is well aware of what he has done and why; he describes his own transformation from committed republican to propagandist for Augustus in merciless terms, also repeating Csokor's key word *Mensch*: 'Ein Mensch war ich damals, der kämpfte . . . Ich finde den Namen des Tieres nicht, mit dem ich mich heute vergleiche. Ein Geier, ein Schakal, ein Schwein – es ist alles zu wenig!'[64] Any of the *Bekenntnisbuch* contributors present among the audience at the gala première must surely have recognized themselves, if they had had but a modicum of Horace's self-awareness – or Csokor's honesty.

In an article that appeared soon after the end of the war, Frederick Lehner characterized Csokor as a 'reiner Tor', because of his unwillingness to compromise in his work, describing him as a writer who wrote 'weil er muß, fern von Sensationen, Bestsellermöglichkeiten und dergleichen äußerer Stimulanz'.[65] His departure from Vienna in 1938 had shown a similar readiness to follow through his beliefs in action. How did he manage to survive in the post-war cross-fire from left and right? From the stance he took against Hitler, one might expect the rigid insistence on principle suggested by Federmann's characterization of him in the *Neue österreichische Biographie*:

> Ebenso wie er es zu verhindern verstand, daß die Verfechter der nationalsozialistischen Ideologie wieder zu Ehren und Würden gelangen konnten, ebenso entschieden wandte er sich gegen die demagogischen Verfechter der kommunistischen Ideologie, die

unter dem Schutz der sowjetischen Besatzungsmacht die öffentliche Meinung zu beeinflussen trachteten.[66]

(It is characteristic that the only example Federmann gives is of the communist danger.) Federmann is taking the principle of *nil nisi bonum* too far; Csokor, despite his idealism, was no *Tor*, even if he managed to remain relatively *rein*. He was well aware of political constraints, as he was aware of the various factors influencing the situation in Austria, and he did compromise where he felt it was necessary or useful. He did not manage to realize his own desire to make the anti-fascist, humanist tradition in Austrian literature the basis for a renewal of literary life, but he did keep the PEN Club together and reasonably independent through difficult times, and he did provide an honourable and dignified official representative for Austrian literature – perhaps more honourable and dignified than it deserved.

Notes

[1] Norbert Langer, *Dichter aus Österreich* (Vienna, 1956), p. 8.

[2] Contributors to the *Bekenntnisbuch* who are dealt with in *Dichter aus Österreich* include: Freiberg, Ginzkey, Grogger, Landgrebe, Mell, Oberkofler, Perkonig, Waggerl, Weinheber, Zerzer.

[3] Langer, *Dichter aus Österreich*, p. 116.

[4] E. J. Görlich and F. Romanik, *Geschichte Österreichs* (Innsbruck, 1970), p. 551.

[5] Ibid.

[6] Robert Neumann, *Deutschland deine Österreicher* (Hamburg, 1970); quoted from Rowohlt Taschenbuch edition, 1974, p. 75.

[7] Hans Georg Behr, *Die österreichische Provokation: ein Mahnruf für Deutsche* (Munich, 1971); quoted from Fischer Taschenbuch edition, 1973, pp. 42–3. How long this official amnesia lasted can be seen in another book published with government support, indeed, published by the *Bundesministerium für Unterricht* in 1970 to celebrate twenty-five years of the Second Republic. The purpose of Karl Gutkas, Alios Brusatti, Erika Weinzierl (eds.), *Österreich 1945–1970: 25 Jahre Zweite Republik* (Vienna, 1970), is, according to the introduction, to make visible 'die Schwierigkeiten und Größe der Aufbauarbeit' and to contribute 'zur Verlebendigung des demokratischen Lebens'. One page of this 364-page book deals with the legislative aspects of the *Nationalsozialistenfrage*, but the only reference to any problem of political attitudes, to any need to come to terms with the past, is hidden

behind the lapidary statement, which is not developed, 'Viel schwieriger fiel den Österreichern die Bewältigung der eigenen jüngsten Vergangenheit, besonders die Ereignisse von 1934.' (47) (This was another book that was sent out to foreign universities.)

8 Ernst Joseph Görlich, *Das Handbuch des Österreichers* (Salzburg, 1949).

9 Kurt Bartsch, 'Die österreichische Gegenwartsliteratur', in V. Zmegac (ed.), *Die Geschichte der deutschen Literatur* (Königstein/Ts, 1984), p. 695.

10 E. Rollett, *Österreichische Gegenwartsliteratur – Aufgabe, Lage, Forderung* (Vienna, 1946); quoted in D. Lyon, J. Marko, E. Staudinger, F. C. Weber (eds.), *Österreich-'bewußt' sein – bewußt Österreicher sein?* (Vienna, 1985), pp. 22–3.

11 See, for example, Carry Hauser, 'Vergessen darf ich nicht', in Jochen Jung (ed.), *Vom Reich zu Österreich: Erinnerungen an Kriegsende und Nachkriegszeit* (Salzburg, 1983); quoted from *dtv* edition (1985), p. 17; also Viktor Matejka's article, 'War 1945 ein Anfang?', in the same volume, pp. 26–7.

12 Herbert Eisenreich, 'Das schöpferische Mißtrauen oder ist Österreichs Literatur eine österreichische Literatur?', written in 1959, published in O. Basil, H. Eisenreich, I. Ivask (eds.), *Das große Erbe: Aufsätze zur österreichischen Literatur* (Graz, 1962); also in H. Eisenreich, *Reaktionen: Essays zur Literatur* (Gütersloh, 1964).

13 E.g. Wilhelm Morawietz, 'Das staatsbürgerliche Bewußtsein in der österreichischen Dichtung', *Österreich in Geschichte und Literatur*, 11 (1967).

14 Jörg Mauthe, *Die große Hitze, oder die Errettung Österreichs durch den Legionsrat Dr. Tuzzi* (Vienna, 1974), p. 111. A very different, more recent, attempt to define what is specifically Austrian about Austrian literature is Robert Menasse's *Die sozialpartnerschaftliche Ästhetik: Das Österreichische an der österreichischen Literatur der Zweiten Republik* (Vienna, 1990). As the title suggests, it is a neo-Marxist explanation, which sees the Austrian organization of capitalism as the 'base' determining the cultural 'superstructure'. It suggests that class conflict has been avoided by absorbing workers' representatives into the system. This view would see the emerging consensus on the 'Austrian Idea' between 1945 and 1955 as a parallel to the socio-economic consensus of the wage and price agreements between 1947 and 1951, which, while presenting the illusion of national unity, in reality sacrificed workers' interests to the re-establishment of capitalism.

15 Görlich, *Handbuch des Österreichers*, p. 214.

16 Ibid., pp. 207–8.

17 A letter of 17 October 1945, in *Turm*, 1 no. 4/5 (1945), p. 109; quoted in F. Aspetsberger, 'Versuchte Korrekturen. Ideologie und Politik im Drama um 1945', in F. Aspetsberger, N. Frei, H. Lengauer (eds.),

Literatur der Nachkriegszeit und der fünfziger Jahre in Österreich (Vienna, 1984), p. 245. See also Doderer's essay of 1954, 'Der Anschluß ist vollzogen', in *Kontinente*, 7 no. 8 (1953–4), 20–3.

18 Görlich, *Handbuch des Österreichers*, p. 324.

19 See Klaus Amann, 'Vorgeschichten. Kontinuitäten in der österreichischen Literatur von den dreißiger zu den fünfziger Jahren', in Aspetsberger, Frei, Lengauer (eds.), *Literatur der Nachkriegszeit*, pp. 46–58.

20 'Kollaborateure der Kultur', *Die Furche*, 23 March 1946; reprinted in J. Kocensky (ed.), *Dokumentation zur österreichischen Zeitgeschichte, 1945–1955* (2nd edn Vienna, 1975), p. 483.

21 One of the Austrian writers who profited most in financial terms from collaboration with the Nazis, Richard Billinger, wrote a play *Das Haus*, first performed in 1949, in which the 'house' symbolizes Austrian tradition and links with the past. The owner's younger brother Max, who returns in the uniform of a US officer and talking about Europe and Europeanism, is described by his brother as an 'Abenteurer, eine haltlose Figur' who missed 'die dunklen Jahre', concluding 'wer das Haus nicht verteidigt . . . verliert es'; the ghost of their mother appears, telling Max to leave the house immediately. Aspetsberger (art. cit., pp. 265–6) comments: 'Csokor wird sich gleich wohl erkannt haben.'

22 Ibid., p. 482.

23 Amann, 'Vorgeschichten', p. 46. The list includes Broch, Brod, Canetti, for example. A complete list of prizes and prizewinners is given in Hans F. Prokop, *Österreichisches Literaturhandbuch* (Vienna, 1974).

24 For *Die Wolfshaut*, see Anthony Bushell, 'A book too soon? Hans Lebert's *Die Wolfshaut* and Austrian *Vergangenheitsbewältigung*', in Bushell (ed.), *Essays in Germanic Studies = Trivium*, 28 (1993), 93–103; for *Fasching* see Robert Menasse, *Die sozialpartnerschaftliche Ästhetik*, pp. 137–43.

25 Ernst Machek (ed.), *Das österreichische Wort: Gedanken und Aussprüche großer Österreicher* (Graz, 1959); another *Buchspende* distributed by Austrian Institutes around the world.

26 Ibid., p. 29.

27 Viktor Suchy, 'Die "österreichische Idee" als konservative Staatsidee bei Hugo von Hofmannsthal, Richard von Schaukal und Anton Wildgans', in Aspetsberger (ed.), *Staat und Gesellschaft in der modernen österreichischen Literatur* (Vienna, 1977), p. 21.

28 Walter Weiß, 'Zwischenbilanz: Österreichische Beiträge zur Gegenwartsliteratur', in Walter Weiß and Sigrid Schmid (eds.), *Zwischenbilanz: Eine Anthologie österreichischer Gegenwartsliteratur* (Salzburg, 1976); quoted from *dtv* edition (Munich, 1978), p. 14. According to Hilde Spiel, this harmony continued into the 1970s; see H. Spiel (ed.),

Kindlers Literaturgeschichte der Gegenwart. Autoren, Werke, Themen, Tendenzen nach 1945: Die zeitgenössische Literatur Österreichs (Zurich/ Munich, 1976), p. 67.

[29] Ibid., p. 27.

[30] Csokor, *Zeuge einer Zeit: Briefe aus dem Exil 1933–1950* (Munich/ Vienna, 1964), p. 25.

[31] See M. R. Mitchell, 'Der Mensch und die Macht: Csokor's attempts to deal with the Third Reich in his plays', in Joseph P. Strelka (ed.), *Immer ist Anfang: Der Dichter Franz Theodor Csokor* (Berne, 1991), pp. 94–6.

[32] Paul Blaha, 'Meine Begenungen mit Franz Theodor Csokor', in Ulrich N. Schulenburg (ed.), *Lebensbilder eines Humanisten: Ein Franz Theodor Csokor-Buch* (Vienna, 1992), pp. 24–5. It should be pointed out that Csokor was not the *mélange adultère de tout* that this suggests. His humanism was not an abstract programme, but focused on individuals, and was combined with an immense capacity for empathy, even with those whose actions he condemned, in whom he could always see the *Mensch* that was the focal point of his outlook.

[33] See Amann, 'Vorgeschichten', pp. 92–3.

[34] C. A. Dawson-Scott, the originator of the idea, quoted in R. A. Wilford, 'The PEN Club, 1930–50', *Journal of Contemporary History*, 14 (1979), 99.

[35] Loc. cit.

[36] Quoted in ibid., footnote 2.

[37] The period of 'pactitis' symbolized by the Treaty of Locarno, 'an alliance,' according to Golo Mann, 'of all with all against all', *The History of Germany since 1789*, tr. Jackson (London, 1968), p. 363.

[38] Amann, 'Vorgeschichten', p. 22.

[39] Csokor, *Zeuge einer Zeit*, p. 177.

[40] Quoted in Amann, 'Vorgeschichten', p. 100.

[41] For a more detailed treatment of the subject, see Dieter Stiefel, *Entnazifierung in Österreich* (Vienna, 1981).

[42] See Amann, 'Vorgeschichten', pp. 93–4.

[43] Rudolf Henz, *Fügung und Widerstand* (Graz, 1963), p. 441; quoted in Amann, 'Vorgeschichten', p. 80.

[44] See Amann, 'Vorgeschichten', pp. 105–19.

[45] Friedrich Heer, 'Nach 1945', in Jochen Jung (ed.), *Vom Reich zu Österreich*, p. 153.

[46] Quoted in Amann, 'Vorgeschichten', p. 127; also in Amann's article in Aspetsberger, Frei, Lengauer (eds.), *Literatur der Nachkriegszeit*, p. 124.

[47] H. Weigel, 'The Jolly Csokor oder Als Zivilist im Kalten Krieg', *Morgen: Monatsschrift freier Akademiker*, 5 (1953), 9–10.

[48] Quoted in Brygida Brandys, 'Franz Theodor Csokor und die Idee einer menschlichen Gesellschaft', in Schulenberg (ed.), *Lebensbilder eines Humanisten*, p. 90.

49 Jethro Bithell, 'Franz Theodor Csokor', *German Life and Letters (GLL)*, 8 no. 1 (1954), p. 37.

50 Langer, *Dichter aus Österreich*, p. 28.

51 *Kalypso* had only six performances in its Burgtheater production; *Der verlorene Sohn* (1947) reached seventeen, *Caesars Witwe* (1955) fourteen.

52 Quoted in Spiel (ed.), *Kindlers Literaturgeschichte*, p. 510.

53 Bithell, loc. cit.

54 Alfred Werner, 'Austrian literature then and now', *GLL*, 2 (1948–9), p. 212.

55 Wolfgang Greisenegger, 'Das Theaterleben nach 1945', in Aspetsberger, Frei, Lengauer (eds.), *Literatur der Nachkriegszeit*, p. 227.

56 It was, for example, put on in Vienna in 1949, 1958, 1966, in Graz in 1955 and in Salzburg in 1956.

57 Csokor, 'Epilog des Autors', *Gottes General. Drama in sieben Stationen* (Hamburg/Vienna, 1956), p. 143.

58 Csokor, *Der verlorene Sohn*, in Csokor, *Europäische Trilogie* (Vienna, 1954), p. 204.

59 Gotthard Böhm, 'Drama in Österreich seit 1945', in Spiel (ed.), *Kindlers Literaturgeschichte*, p. 507.

60 And drew appropriately approving comments from those who had previously attacked him as a fellow-traveller. See Torberg's review, republished in Friedrich Torberg, *Das fünfte Rad am Thespiskarren* (Munich, 1966), pp. 249–50.

61 Csokor, *Caesars Witwe*, in *Olymp und Golgotha: Trilogie einer Weltwende* (Hamburg, 1954), pp. 18 and 20 (N.B. each play in the trilogy has separate pagination).

62 Ibid., p. 45.

63 Ibid., p. 64.

64 Ibid., p. 24.

65 Frederick Lehner, 'Literatur in Exil: Franz Theodor Csokor', *German Quarterly*, 20, no. 4 (1947), 210.

66 Reinhard Federmann in *Neue österreichische Biographie: Ab 1815*, vol. 19 (Vienna, 1977), p. 46.

5

Remembering and Forgetting:
Hilde Spiel's *Rückkehr nach Wien* in 1946

ANDREA HAMMEL

Dates always pose difficulties for literature. The title of this volume, *Austria, 1945–1955*, is no exception. The Austrian-born writer and journalist Hilde Spiel visited Austria for the first time, after ten years in exile in Britain, between 30 January and 23 February 1946 under the auspices of the British forces as a 'war correspondent' for the *New Statesman*. These dates are clearly set out in her published diary *Rückkehr nach Wien: Ein Tagebuch*.[1] This work has a complicated history. Back in London shortly after her visit to Vienna she wrote, 'mit Hilfe meiner Tagebuchnotizen, der unmittelbare Eindruck noch abrufbar',[2] an English manuscript entitled 'The Streets of Vineta', but this was never published in English. In the 1960s she eventually translated this manuscript into German. An extract appeared in the *Frankfurter Allgemeine Zeitung* on 2 September 1964 under the same title. The book *Rückkehr nach Wien* – first published by the Nymphenburger Verlagshandlung in Munich – includes a postscript dated September 1967 which describes her life back in London in the year 1946 and was obviously not part of the original manuscript.

For a diary such a delayed publication might not be too uncommon, but the situation illuminates the problems of literature in exile and by exiles in general. It also poses difficult questions for the definition of exile literature as an area of study. To restrict the study of exile literature to works written between 1933 and 1945, which had been the initial tendency of researchers, has been rejected during more recent years. *Rückkehr nach Wien* shows how torn Hilde Spiel still was between Britain and Austria despite her naturalization and her 'assimilated rank' of major in the British forces. On the one hand Spiel feels doubly at home: 'Im britischen Pressequartier des dritten Wiener Gemeindebezirks bin ich auf doppelter Weise daheim.'[3] But the places of her childhood exert a strong spell over her. She frequently reflects on these forces of memory with great care and stylistic skill, which even induces one literary critic to call her a 'Viennese female Proust'.[4] Spiel describes, for example, her deliberate attempts to distance herself from her birthplace, Vienna, the memories of her youth and the Austrian landscape. Asked why she is hesitating to go on a trip to Kärnten, she answers: 'Warum wirklich nicht? Wenn es nicht eine heimliche, unheimliche Angst ist, daß in Kärnten meine Kräfte zur Distanzierung mich völlig verlassen.'[5]

She returned to London and her emotional ambiguities concerning both countries remained. These are made especially clear in the letters from Austria to her husband in London.[6] Her visit to Austria was only half home-coming; it was also a move towards a new kind of exile. She had to deal with the fact that there was a gap between her and those who stayed behind in Vienna whether they had or had not been involved in the National Socialist takeover. She was similarly divided in loyalty on her return to London. *Rückkehr nach Wien* thus extends the parameter of exile literature showing that the phenomenon did not suddenly cease in 1945 after the death threat to the Jewish population in Europe had been lifted and a life in exile away from Germany and Austria was no longer absolutely vital.

The route of the initial manuscript to publication illustrates how its history is intrinsically linked with the problem of language. The Viennese writer, Martina Wied, who also spent her exile in Great Britain, wrote four novels there, but as she always wrote in German they were not published until the end of the Second World War and her return to Austria.[7] Hermynia Zur Mühlen, another Austrian-born exile writing in Britain, switched languages and wrote three novels in English. Consequently these were not published in German for a long time: *Als der Fremde kam*, the German translation of *Came the Stranger*, only appeared in print in 1994.[8]

Hilde Spiel arrived in London in 1936 speaking English reasonably well but unable to understand less educated people and, of course, unable to write professionally in English. *Flute and Drums*,[9] which was published in London by Hutchinson in 1939 and which deals with the events during her stay in Italy in 1936, was originally written in German but translated into English by Spiel herself with the help of her husband, the writer and journalist Peter de Mendelsohn, and a friend, Eric Dancy. After this enterprise de Mendelsohn, who had mastered the language switch himself and at that point expected to stay in Britain permanently, encouraged her to start writing in English.[10] This change in language was mirrored by a change in genre: Waltraud Strickhausen[11] argues that Spiel's *Lebensbruch* was paralleled by a creative *Schaffensbruch*, and that she almost exclusively wrote essays instead of prose fiction over the next two decades. She cites four reasons for this development: firstly, linguistic difficulties, secondly, a different audience, thirdly, a change in intention of her literary expression, and, last but by no means least, the material conditions of literary production. Strickhausen describes the greater ease with which essays could be sold for publication, but what is not often noted is that Spiel had two children and one miscarriage during the war. Her daughter Christine was born in 1939, and her son Felix was born in 1944, with a miscarriage in between. Obviously, writing shorter essays could be fitted around child care and housework with fewer difficulties. Her exile in England coincided with her development from a young student and writer without many ties and responsibilities into a wife and a mother of two who had to earn a living.

Although it is correct to say that Spiel did not publish any longer works of prose between *Flute and Drums* and *The Darkened Room* published in 1961,[12] she did write *The Fruits of Prosperity*,[13] which was printed in the exile publication *Die Zeitung* in 1941, as well as the manuscript 'The Streets of Vineta'. All the three latter works were written in English first and later translated into German by Spiel herself. This procedure poses an intriguing methodological question for the researcher: which version is the master text – the English version written by a native German-speaker in her second language or the German translation? It also shows that the process of reintegration into Austrian cultural life after 1945 was fraught with difficulties.

Since only the German version of *Rückkehr nach Wien* has ever been published, and Spiel's unpublished manuscripts, which were acquired by the Österreichische Nationalbibliothek in 1991,[14] are not yet accessible, the interesting comparison between the

English manuscript and the German version will have to wait. But there is already more than one linguistic twist inherent in the return to Vienna by an Austrian-born naturalized-British exile, especially if the exile, as Spiel did, visited Vienna under the aegis of the British Allied Forces and lived in the British Press Quarters. For a correspondent to be an exiled Austrian seems to have been the norm rather than the exception, judging from the casual comments which Spiel's statement that she had been born in Vienna provokes from a Reuters news agency official. Hilde Spiel illuminates her linguistic return in poignant prose:

> Benommen sage ich Margaret und der Sergeantin adieu, verspreche die eine wiederzusehen und lasse die andere für immer in der irrealen Welt des britischen Armeelebens versinken.
>   Mein Gepäck wird zugleich zum Gegenstand aufgeregter Unterhaltung in meiner Muttersprache, mit vielen Wendungen, die mir inzwischen entfallen sind. Als Empfangschef, Portier und Träger sich um mich scharen, entfliehe ich ihrer allzu lauten Wirklichkeit in den Lift.[15]

Spiel feels more at home with at least some of the members of the British forces, but realizes that here in Vienna the British world is unreal. Deciding where her loyalties lie is much easier for her on her stopover in Frankfurt in Germany. There she sees the misery of immediate post-war Germany – cripples, starving children and the empty looks from prostitutes – and the wall of hatred reminds her 'daß diese deutsche Tragödie nicht die unsere ist'.[16] This is true for Spiel from her viewpoint as a British national as well as an Austrian-born exile. In Germany the places she visits are not inherently linked with childhood memories and their mother tongue is not quite her mother tongue. But from the moment Spiel sets eyes on the ski slopes of the Wienerwald and hears the forgotten 'Wendungen' in her mother tongue, her journey takes on a different meaning from an ordinary trip by a journalist.

Her prophecy, however, that she will inevitably glorify her childhood is only partly true. On her trip to Heiligenstadt she follows the traces of her childhood: driving down the cobbles of the Döblinger Hauptstraße she finds the area still largely unchanged. Even the occasional newly painted house front, indicating that this building was occupied by the American Allied Forces, does not disturb the general picture of familiarity.

> Verträumt wie eh und jeh schaukeln diese kleinen Blumenläden, Konditoreien, Papiergeschäfte auf den Wogen der Zeit.
> Jede Gasse, jede Ecke ist mir vertraut. In diesem Bezirk, dem neunzehnten, war seit Generationen die Familie meiner Mutter daheim. Fast in jedem Haus lebte eine ihrer Tanten, einer ihrer Onkels und Vettern. Dort drüben wohnte meine Großmutter Melanie.[17]

But these descriptions are not only romantic nostalgia, for Spiel immediately connects the places and the people with their historical context. Her grandmother's life is described as *fin-de-siècle* tragedy and Spiel evokes her own 1920s youth with a description of a local attic and its liberating atmosphere of gramophone concerts, portrait painting and secret meetings for two. It soon becomes apparent that Spiel leaves out the recent past when describing her visit: her grandmother's story is continued in as much as she was an unhappily married woman who thought herself mistreated by everybody and negatively influenced her children's lives. But in this early entry dated 6 February, Spiel does not mention Großmutter Melanie's own unhappy end, her death after nine weeks in Theresienstadt.

On this specific visit Spiel avoids the most painful memories and tries to recapture the innocence of her childhood. This becomes manifest in her rejection of her present role as a member of the British forces. She sends the driver and the jeep away and leaves her military coat and her shoulder bag behind. 'Dieses letzte Wegstück bin ich lieber unbeschwert.'[18] Again this does not mean timeless glorification: her memory goes further back and she remembers her early childhood living with her parents in Kraków. Her father was then a young officer in the Habsburg army where the officer's servants spoke with half a dozen different accents and all sang 'Gott erhalte' at dinner parties. At the same time she remembers her horror at the begging children in the Polish town who were dispersed by the coachman with his whip, and at the way in which her family lost its income and status when her father was decommissioned.

Instead of the persecution of her family because of her Jewish background, she remembers her first communion and the processions. In *Rückkehr nach Wien* Spiel describes how she kneels crying in the church of her native area of Vienna, which more than any explanation illuminates the warped racial laws of the National Socialist regime. Still the genocide is not openly discussed. This might have been because of a variety of reasons – the focus of this diary on her return to her birthplace, the refusal to discuss the Jewish population always as victims, and her general reluctance to discuss the indescribable horror in detail.

For Spiel, Vienna and her early life were not primarily connected with Jewishness. Although her family were descended from Sephardic Jews and her ancestors included *Oberlandesrabbiner*, they had been converted Catholics for several generations. Spiel writes in her memoirs: 'Daß der Glaube meiner Vorväter nicht der meine war, blieb mir als Kind unbekannt.'[19] When emotions overcome her in the church, Spiel describes them as suppressed 'Kummer um die Erniedrigung meiner Heimat',[20] the worries about her children during the war and the grief about the death of her father, and not as a response to the National Socialist mass murder of Middle European Jewry.

Although never uncritical of Vienna's history and the history of the Austrian Empire in general, Spiel insists that there have been moments in this history where a multicultural harmony was at least attempted. In *Die Früchte des Wohlstands*, which is set in Vienna during a period of great economic expansion in the 1870s and 1880s, Spiel describes the coexistence of the nations under Habsburg rule in down-to-earth metaphors. The young Croat Milan comes to seek his luck in Vienna, and after some aberrations he joins the firm of a textile merchant with a Jewish background and marries the merchant's daughter Stephanie. His jovial approach contributes to the success of the business, which is in turn a mirror for the economic and political success of the Austrian Empire. When Milan goes out with his business acquaintances from all corners of the Empire, it sounds like the ideal multicultural society:

> Milan war mit den Oberösterreichern bei ihrem Most gesessen, mit den Waldviertlern bei ihrem Trebernschnaps und mit den Mähren bei ihrem Bier. Er hatte den goldenen Gewürztraminer der südtirolerischen Provinzen nicht minder freudig genossen als den roten Karlowitzer seiner Heimat. Die ungarischen Süßweine, die polnischen Liköre hatten ihm gleichermaßen gemundet.[21]

Konstanze Fliedl argues that Spiel insists on 'a "natural"

homogeneity . . . in the monarchy'[22] and that she ignores the conflicts between the imperial provinces. While Spiel uses these
images as a background, it should be noted that *Die Früchte des
Wohlstands* is also a novel more specifically about Vienna. In connection with life in the city Spiel describes the conflicts between
the citizens coming from many different backgrounds. Obviously
the integration of the Jewish families plays a vital part. Spiel
clearly illuminates the double discrimination from which both
the uneducated young Croat and the cultured Jewish woman
suffer. In addition both have rather prejudiced views towards
each other. The city of Vienna with its liberal arts and entertain-
ments is part of the attraction and part of the problem. In the last
chapter a return to Croatia is offered to Milan and his young
family, both as an escape and as an impossibility. The novel ends
with the burning of the Ringtheater in 1881, in which both Milan
and Stephanie perish. This seems to mark the end of a relatively
peaceful period both for the different Habsburg provinces and
the Jewish population.

During her return in 1946 certain features of Vienna remind
Hilde Spiel of the successes in the Austro-Jewish symbioses. It
becomes repeatedly clear that, for Spiel, one of the worst crimes
of the National Socialist regime was the negation of a relationship between the Jews and the Austrian state. In an interview for
the German TV series for ZDF, *Zeugen des Jahrhunderts*, with
Anna Linsel in August 1988, Spiel suggests – taking Franz Theodor Csokor's play *Dritter November 1918* as an example – that the
Jewish part of the Austrian population had perhaps been the
only ones which felt a real duty to the Austrian state because
most of the other Austrian citizens would claim to have their
roots in Slovenia or Istria or Tyrol and only the assimilated Jews
identified themselves primarily as Austrian nationals.[23]

Edward Timms points out that 'for the upwardly mobile Jew
in the process of emancipation, the prestige of German culture
was so great that Berlin, Vienna, Prague and other rapidly expand-
ing cities became the centres of a remarkable cultural affluence'.[24]
Spiel wanted to remind herself of the cultural achievements of
the Viennese Jews, and it became one of her main aims to re-
instate these into Austrian cultural politics. Her work about
Fanny von Arnstein was a major achievement in that respect.[25]
She wanted to differentiate between different members of the

Jewish population. In *Rückkehr nach Wien* it soon becomes clear that she herself was part of a very assimilated group of Jews. Returning to her old house she describes all the inhabitants and their various abodes. In the cellar of her old house there used to live a Galician Jew whose situation is part of Spiel's half-romantic description of times past. Yet Spiel is more interested in the non-Jewish inhabitants, some of whom became Nazis, than in a Jewish fate which must have been so different from hers from beginning to end.

In the interview with Anna Linsel she is asked about her attitude towards the sculptor Alfred Hrdlicka, who had created a sculpture of a Jew washing the streets. Spiel thinks that this is an unsuitable memorial as it depicts the Jew in a degrading situation: 'Ich meine aber was den Menschen eingeprägt werden sollte, sind die großen Figuren des Judentums: Einstein, Freud.'[26] This is a completely understandable sentiment, but what is more difficult to comprehend is her clandestine acceptance of social hierarchy which assumes the superiority of the assimilated Jew: 'man hat heute keine Vorstellung mehr von der Hierarchie, die auch im Judentum geherrscht hat, von den vielen Stufen und Schattierungen dieser Menschen – die werden jetzt alle in einen Topf geworfen.'[27]

This is another indicator of how hard it was for Hilde Spiel to sympathize with 'the Jews' in general. Personally she found it easier to put herself in the position of a liberal, educated non-Jew. Spiel admits that one of the reasons why she emigrated relatively early was her fear of her own willingness to compromise. She repeatedly calls the time between the uprising in 1934 and Hitler's annexation of Austria 'eine verschmierte' or 'schlampige Zeit'. Her judgement of those involved with the National Socialist regime is therefore also inconsistent. Her post-war admiration for Heimito von Doderer and Alexander Lernet-Holenia has often been commented on. She admitted that they all knew about Doderer's temporary acceptance of anti-Semitism but that they never talked about it. Spiel seems to have found it easier to forgive a man like Doderer who changed his mind than a man like an unnamed newspaper editor who had been opposed to the regime but still remained in Austria, continued in his post and even joined the NSDAP allegedly to cover for his friends. In an entry for 9 February, Spiel judges him harshly and accuses him of just being another cog in the National Socialist state machinery. She especially mocks his verbal opposition: 'Einmal wöchentlich besprach er mit gleichgesinnten Freunden . . . die Vulgarität des Regimes.'[28] This kind of intellectual opposition from a person in a relatively safe position and the discussion of the horrors of National Socialism are shown as useless responses. It has to be noted that Spiel finds people who claimed after the war that they had been against the National Socialists all along but who in fact colluded with the regime far more despicable than those who made mistakes but at least did not claim to have been in the opposition. Spiel admits, however, that it is often not very clear-cut and that her resolution – made when still in London – not to shake hands with anybody who had been in any way implicated was impossible to adhere to. It also becomes clear that Hilde Spiel is not in favour of discussing publicly the atrocities committed under Hitler.

There are several reasons for this stance. Firstly, there is the inadequacy of language. In her entry for 9 February she describes her visit to the Count and Countess P., who live in the Soviet-occupied zone of Vienna. Their dilapidated palace and its furniture and decor had been wilfully destroyed by the Soviet soldiers. The couple are torn between their past grandeur and their present misery. Spiel shows how the countess's complaints about rapes of local women by Soviet soldiers sound ridiculously inadequate:

> 'Alle Frauen in diesem Haus. Die Grünzeughändlerin gleich dreimal. Ich meine, sowas gehört sich doch nicht. Ich meine, das ist doch Privatsache, finden Sie nicht?'
> Hilflos, hilflos wie ihre Worte, die der unerhörten Realität nicht gewachsen sind.[29]

Hilde Spiel has never tried to write directly about the murder of the European Jewry and any of the other atrocities of the Nazi regime. Indeed, she insists that realism would be an inadequate tool for dealing with the subject. Her narrative style and her essayistic technique do not lend themselves to an open discussion of mass murder. But it is also her expressed opinion that such a discussion would do more harm than good. Asked about hidden anti-Semitism in Austria in the 1980s, and especially about the Waldheim debate, Spiel states:

Ich bin der Meinung, das hätte nicht alles unter dem Teppich her-
vorgekehrt werden müssen, weil es keine kollektive Analyse
gibt, Reinigung durch Analyse wie in der privaten psychoter-
apeutischen Therapie. Ich glaube nicht, . . . das man es aus der
Welt schafft, indem man es ans Tageslicht zerrt . . . Gewisse
dunkle Regungen im kollektiven Unterbewußten sollte man dort
ruhen lassen und nicht wecken.[30]

Secondly, Spiel realizes that it is difficult to judge guilt and in the
end she cannot even reject the newspaper editor Stefan B.: 'Ich
kann ihn nicht verurteilen, denn ich bin in seinem Lager, im
Lager der Lebenden, die den Toten überlegen sind.'[31] During her
stay in Berlin she is intrigued by the continuity between the Hitler
period and post-war Germany. Her blonde hairdresser, Brigitte,
who used to attend to the wives of the National Socialist élite,
now does the hair of the women from the Allied armies. Even
with their own numerous housekeepers, Spiel and her husband
do not check on their past in National Socialist Germany. Spiel
only seems concerned with their present loyalties and takes it for
granted that it would be impossible for them still to believe in
National Socialism after the disastrous end of the war.

In *Die hellen und die finsteren Zeiten* she constructs an answer to
Friedrich Torberg's question about the guilty and the innocent as
follows: 'Der Prüfstein, meine ich, könnte sein, was mit jemand
geschehen wäre und wie er sich verhalten hätte, wenn Hitler
siegreich gewesen wäre und Österreich für immer einem deutsch
dominierten Europa einverleibt.'[32] An individual's commitment
to an Austrian national identity separate from Germany is Hilde
Spiel's main principle on which to measure a person's accept-
ability. This view plays a major part in both her emotional and
her intellectual life. She admits that his essential Austrianness
was the major feature which fascinated her about her second
husband, Hans Flesch von Brunningen. It also played a part in
her admiration for Doderer and Lernet-Holenia.

Because of the lack of opposition to Hitler's annexation of
Austria from either inside or outside, the emphasis of Austrians
in exile in London was placed on reminding the international
community of its distinct political and cultural identity. There
was no Austrian government in exile so the Free Austrian Movement in London, which by the end of 1943 represented over 7,000

members, subscribed to the aim of publicizing Austrian culture. Despite Hilde Spiel's attempts to integrate as much as possible into British cultural life and her contempt for the infighting within the exile organizations, she supported the same aims. A member of the Austrian PEN Club in exile, she was on the list of Austrian participants of the XVIIth International PEN Congress in September 1941 in London. Klaus Amann argues in his book, *P.E.N. Politik – Emigration – Nationalsozialismus*, that the Austrian PEN in exile identified explicitly from the end of 1941 onwards with the aims of the Free Austrian Movement.[33]

The Moscow Declaration on Austria, released on 30 October 1943, in which the governments of the United Kingdom, the Soviet Union and the United States of America stated that Austria had been the first free country to fall victim to Hitler's aggression and that they were committed to a free and independent Austria, was an immensely important document to Hilde Spiel. In her only work in which she deals with exile in London, *Anna und Anna*,[34] the Moscow Declaration is included in part in its original form as a film script. The film project was never realized but when *Anna und Anna* was performed as a play in the Burgtheater in Vienna with Claus Peymann directing, Spiel insisted on the inclusion of the whole Moscow Declaration.

In her interview with Anna Linsel, Spiel also points out how important the last paragraph of the declaration was to her. 'Austria is reminded, however, that she has a responsibility which she cannot evade for participation in the war on the side of Hitlerite Germany, and that in the final settlement account will inevitably be taken of her own contribution to her liberation.'[35] The fact that the Austrians' participation in their liberation was rather limited is made clear in *Rückkehr nach Wien*. When she returns to the Cafe Herrenhof, the head waiter greets her with the same whining monologue a friend experienced before her:

> 'Der Herr Doktor haben den Krieg im Ausland verbracht?' würde der Kellner ihn auf jede höfliche indirekte Weise fragen, die seit Maria Theresia im Schwange ist. 'Das war aber gescheit vom Herr Doktor. Da haben 'S sich viel Unannehmlichkeiten erspart. Wenn der Herr Doktor wüßten, was uns alles passiert ist. Das Elend, das wir durchgemacht haben. Wie gut der Herr Doktor aussehen – wirklich, eine Freud!'

> Enteignung, Demütigung, Verhaftung und Todesgefahr, ille-
> gale Flucht über versperrte Grenzen, Jahre des Exils, ein feind-
> licher Ausländer in einem vom Krieg zerrütteten Land – all das
> würde zunichte werden, würde sich in Luft auflösen, mit einem
> Fingerschnalzen weggeweht.[36]

This gap between the *Daheimgebliebenen* and the *Ausgewanderten*
is one which Spiel has discussed again and again in her writing.
Only in *Anna und Anna* was there a happy ending. In real life
Spiel believed that the differences between the two camps never
completely ceased to exist.[37] During her first stay in Vienna she
tries to explain – when asked to come back to live in Austria –
that she is leading a different life now, that her children were
born in London and that she has ties there as well. In a letter to
her husband she writes that she would never want to be a
Viennese again, that she likes the architecture and the town but
that staying in Vienna is only possible for her in conjunction with
the British.

> Ich bin überzeugt, daß die einzige Chance der Österreicher in
> ihrem ungeheuren Talent für alle Künste liegt, ihrem außeror-
> dentlich guten Geschmack und ihrer künstlerischen Sensitivität.
> Wenn sie lernen, sich zurückzuhalten und die Politik anderen zu
> überlassen, haben sie eine Zukunft in Europa.[38]

This statement has a double significance in view of other parts
of the diary. It is clear that Spiel only gets a sense of renewal in
Austrian life when she meets other intellectuals and artists. She
visits the councillor responsible for Vienna's cultural life, Victor
Mateijka, and feels a new wind blowing through his department.
He became a communist in Dachau and many of his colleagues
lived through the same concentration camp. Ernst Fischer as education minister tries to provide an atmosphere for re-education.
At other gatherings with young artists, though, Spiel experiences
a feeling of *déjà vu*. The abstract drawings a young man shows
his friends, like the whole of the modernism of these young
Austrians, seems to her nothing but a negation of National
Socialist provincial thinking. Compared with the British journals
like *Horizon* and *New Writing*, young Austrian art does not seem
very original. Nevertheless, Spiel believes that there is room for
development within these artists and writers.

Subconsciously her sense of repetition must also connect the attempts of this generation with the failures of her own generation. The reviewer of *Rückkehr nach Wien* for *The Times Literary Supplement* (12 September 1968) points out that the rulers of the late Habsburg Empire tolerated 'a broad spectrum of inventiveness in every field that diverted the attention of the middle classes from concentrating too much on politics'.[39] The author Hilde Spiel cannot be called apolitical – indeed it has often been pointed out that her characters are too much a representation of their times – but in her letter to her husband in London she seems to advocate the possibility of an apolitical cultural re-emergence. On the other hand, the scene with the bespectacled young men and the idolizing young women reminds her not only of the positive atmosphere of her own youth but also of an idealistic young woman, Annie Gadoll, who was killed by the National Socialists. The depiction of these hopeful, left-wing youngsters setting off the memory of her friend whose fate she is only told at that party serves as an antidote to the 'unique mixture of social and cultural, especially musical, and political snobbishness that runs through Miss Spiel's diary'.[40]

The second part of Hilde Spiel's autobiography is entitled *Welche Welt ist meine Welt?*, a question which is symptomatic of her whole life and work. Not only was she torn between countries, not only did her first return to Vienna foretell her eventual return to the country of her birth but she was also always in a torn position in her own cultural *métier*. When she evokes moments of cultural symbiosis between the Jews and the Catholics, and also between the thirteen nations of the Empire, as she did in *Früchte des Wohlstands*, there are moments of both myth-making and clarifying political analysis. In *Fanny von Arnstein oder die Emanzipation* she shows the life of a Jewish woman as an expression of her times but, although she argues that she was not fascinated by her as a figure in her own right, the choice of subject and the end-product leave one to doubt this. In *Rückkehr nach Wien* Spiel is drawn towards the remembering of the historical myth, the forgetting of certain parts of the past and the elucidation of past and present Austrian identity.

Notes

[1] Hilde Spiel, *Rückkehr nach Wien. Ein Tagebuch* (Frankfurt am Main, 1991).

[2] Hilde Spiel, *Die hellen und die finsteren Zeiten. Erinnerungen 1911–1946* (Reinbek, 1991), p. 226.

[3] Spiel, *Rückkehr nach Wien*, p. 29.

[4] In 'Return to Vienna', *The Times Literary Supplement*, 12 September 1968.

[5] Spiel, *Rückkehr nach Wien*, p. 110.

[6] Spiel, *Die hellen und die finsteren Zeiten*, pp. 234ff.

[7] Martina Wied, *Das Einhorn* (Vienna, 1948); *Das Krähennest* (Vienna, 1951); *Die Geschichte des reichen Jünglings* (Innsbruck, 1952); *Der Ehering* (Innsbruck, 1954).

[8] Hermynia Zur Mühlen, *We Poor Shadows* (London, 1943); *Came the Stranger* (London, 1946); *Als der Fremde kam* (Vienna, 1994).

[9] Hilde Spiel, *Flute and Drums* (London, 1939).

[10] Richard Dove, 'The gift of tongues: German-speaking novelists writing in English', in William Abbey *et al.* (eds.), *Between Two Languages: German-speaking Exiles in Great Britain 1933–1945* (Stuttgart, 1995), p. 106.

[11] Waltraud Strickhausen, 'Im Zwiespalt zwischen Literatur und Publizistik', in Claus-Dieter Krohn *et al.* (eds.), *Exilforschung Ein Internationales Jahrbuch*, Band 7, Publizistik im Exil und andere Themen (Munich, 1989), pp. 167–83.

[12] Hilde Spiel, *The Darkened Room* (London, 1961).

[13] Hilde Spiel, 'Fruits of Prosperity', *Die Zeitung* (London, 1941).

[14] See entry for Spiel, Hilde, in Murray G. Hall *et al.*, *Handbuch der Nachlässe und Sammlungen österreichischer Autoren* (Vienna, 1995).

[15] Spiel, *Rückkehr nach Wien*, p. 19.

[16] Ibid., p. 13.

[17] Ibid., p. 44.

[18] Ibid., p. 46.

[19] Spiel, *Die hellen und die finsteren Zeiten*, p. 32.

[20] Spiel, *Rückkehr nach Wien*, p. 49.

[21] Hilde Spiel, *Die Früchte des Wohlstands* (Frankfurt am Main, 1991), p. 139.

[22] Konstanze Fliedl, 'Hilde Spiel's linguistic rights of residence', in E. Timms and R. Robertson (eds.), *Austrian Exodus* (Austrian Studies 6, Edinburgh, 1995), p. 125.

[23] Hilde Spiel in an interview with Anna Linsel, published as *Zeugen des Jahrhunderts: Hilde Spiel Grande Dame* (Göttingen, 1992), pp. 36–7.

[24] Edward Timms, 'Preface' to Timms and Robertson (eds.), *Austrian Exodus*, p. xi.

[25] Hilde Spiel, *Fanny von Arnstein oder die Emanzipation* (Frankfurt am Main, 1978).

[26] Spiel, in the interview *Hilde Spiel Grande Dame*, p. 97.

[27] Ibid.

[28] Spiel, *Rückkehr nach Wien*, p. 73.

[29] Ibid., p. 59.

[30] Spiel, in the interview *Hilde Spiel Grande Dame*, p. 92.

[31] Spiel, *Rückkehr nach Wien*, p. 84.

[32] Spiel, *Die hellen und die finsteren Zeiten*, p. 238.

[33] Klaus Amann, *P.E.N. Politik – Emigration – Nationalsozialismus Ein österreichischer Schriftstellerclub* (Vienna, 1984), p. 71.

[34] Published as Hilde Spiel, *Anna und Anna* (Vienna, 1989).

[35] Quoted from the Moscow Declaration, 30 October 1943, in George E. Berkley, *Vienna and its Jews* (Cambridge, MA, 1988), p. 333.

[36] Spiel, *Rückkehr nach Wien*, pp. 69–70.

[37] Spiel in the interview *Hilde Spiel Grande Dame*, p. 79.

[38] Spiel, *Die hellen und die finsteren Zeiten*, p. 236.

[39] *The Times Literary Supplement*, 12 September 1968.

[40] Ibid.

6

Giraffe unter Palmen:
Saiko's 'Geschichten vom Mittelmeer'

STUART LOW

Critical reaction to Saiko's prose fiction during his lifetime was characterized principally by the disjunction between the high praise extended to it by distinguished contemporary Austrian writers and the uneasy and spasmodic response by the academic establishment.[1] In recent years, it has attracted closer scholarly attention, which in general confirms the contemporary view that Saiko belongs in the first rank of modern Austrian writers.[2]

It is not surprising, and indeed quite proper, that most of this attention has focused on his two major works – the novels *Auf dem Floß* and *Der Mann im Schilf* (and to a lesser extent, the two novellas *Die Klauen des Doppeladlers* and *Die Badewanne*, published together under the title *Der Opferblock*), since they bear directly or obliquely on the post-Habsburg, pre-*Anschluß* political and social condition of Austria; these works form part of the literary 'documentation' of that problematic historical period, not least in terms of their (controversial) contribution towards an understanding of its psychology. A balanced assessment of Saiko's literary achievement, however, must require that, intrinsic merit apart, his volume of stories *Giraffe unter Palmen*, the last of only four major prose publications and therefore a significant part of his œuvre, should receive more commensurate consideration.[3] This collection recalls the fact that Saiko's first published work was itself a short story – *Das letzte Ziel* – which appeared as far back as 1913 in *Der Brenner*. As he states in a posthumously published essay: 'Vielleicht gehört es zu Saikos Affinität mit dem Angelsächsischen, daß ihn neben der Epik "langen Atems" vor allem die Kurzgeschichte interessiert.'[4]

Saiko was not a prolific creative writer, but the explanation for his failure to produce more work in the genre may lie in the priority he accorded to the two novels, given his view of the central cultural importance of the modern novel tradition and his own high sense of mission as a successor in the line of Joyce, Broch and Faulkner. He makes clear, however, in the same essay that he considers his work in the short form to be of a high order: 'Saikos Kurzgeschichten bestehen . . . jeden Vergleich, auch mit den englischen Meisterleistungen dieses Genres.'[5] He provides no clue as to the possible source material of the stories other than that they were the product of a number of holidays spent in Italy after the war – 'Diese Kurzgeschichten spielen mit Vorliebe am Mittelmeer, besonders in Italien (Saikos Geständnis: 'In manchen Landschaften Italiens bin ich glücklich – so weit ein Mensch das von sich sagen kann')'.[6] During his final years, Saiko was working on a third novel, given the provisional title *Murazzo*, which survives only in fragmentary form. The image of the *murazzo*, a defensive sea-dyke, recurs in this collection, and it may be that the stories were a by-product of his studies for that larger work. Italy provides the background to all but one of them, although a specific location (Venice) is identified in only two.

The first (and perhaps the most accomplished) of the stories, *Giraffe unter Palmen*, which lends its title to the collection, is an account of a transitional moment in the life of a fisherman in an impoverished Italian village. Brogio's wife Betta is dying, and her place as housekeeper has been taken over by a woman from the village, Letizia. Betta desperately resists her inevitable replacement, domestically and sexually, by Letizia. She commands Brogio to swear 'bei der Barke San Cristoforo' – the means of his livelihood – that he will dismiss Letizia after Betta's death. The narrative implies that her motive includes sexual jealousy and the fear that her replacement by Letizia will rob her life of its significance. It is structured on two narrative voices: that of the narrator who, with the sparest of means, provides the context and the account of the events, and that of Letizia's unspoken thoughts. Brogio's reactions are not revealed directly, but must be inferred from other sources – namely, his sensitivity towards his wife's condition and her dying wishes, his sense of propriety in regard to the public observation of the rituals of death in this small community, his awareness of the new sexual relationship which will follow his release from Betta and that he will soon return to the fishing which he has neglected during Betta's illness. Through Letizia, the central figure, Saiko demonstrates with remarkable plasticity the urgency of physical attraction which threatens rational control; as she stands by to dry Brogio's body after washing, she almost faints at the sight of its sheer masculinity and, in particular, of the tattoo, depicting a giraffe among palm trees, on his upper arm, which moves – 'ein furchtbar lebendiges Ding' (31) – with the movement of the muscles. *Giraffe* is one of four stories in the collection which focus on female sexuality from the woman's perspective, presented here in terms of irresistible drive and the desire for the surrender and transcendence of self in physical union: in addition to the 'living' giraffe with its obvious phallic significance, there is the sexual symbolism of a second tattoo which depicts a lion holding 'das blutende Herz in den Pranken, ein menschliches Herz, ohne Zweifel das Herz einer Frau . . .'(31) The controlling image of masculinity-as-power is extended by the symbol of the *murazzo* – the great 'Steindamm gegen das Meer' which is reinforced 'mit manneshohen Lavablöcken' (29), and associated with the massive, indestructible figure of Brogio himself – the 'dicke(n) Säule aus braunem haarigem Mannsfleich' (31) – and with Brogio's boat, which is immobilized until released by the death of Betta. For Letizia it also symbolizes both flight from the present, unresolved situation, and also the certainty of that resolution: 'Die Barke San Cristoforo glitt dahin auf den gekräuselten Wogen, und San Cristoforo selbst segnete die Fahrt, die schon beinahe ein Flug war, dorthin, wo es keine Träume mehr braucht, weil sie längst Ereignis und Wirklichkeit sind.'(31) The economic hardship and the struggle for existence is echoed in the starkly reduced physical environment:

> Seit die gefährdeten Stellen des Murazzo, des großen Steindammes gegen das Meer, mit mannshohen Lavablöcken verstärkt waren, gab es keine Überflutungen mehr. Die drei Betonkisten am Fischerhafen waren in Sicherheit, jede zwei Stockwerke hoch, pompejanischrot, maisgelb und indigoblau, schmutzig und abgeblättert, alle drei mit graurosa Jalousien. Weil die paar Tamariskenbäume vor dem Kai zu dünn und kümmerlich waren, gingen die Wäscheschnüre von den Balkonen hinunter zu den zwei Masten von Brogios Barke, die verwahrlost am Ufer lag. (29)

But the continuity of life, its regeneration, is affirmed and
guaranteed by the masculine principle on which the story is
structured. Narrative tension is generated on three levels: by the
conflict of man and environment, by the Brogio–Letizia–Betta
relationship, and, more subtly, by the conflicting demands of the
sexual imperative, on the one hand, and the cultural imperative
of decorum and propriety on the other – the dying Betta must be
accorded her due, and therefore Brogio and Letizia must wait for
her, and their, release and the sanction of the community. Brogio
acknowledges this when, with unconscious irony, he pays tribute
to Letizia's friendship, as they return from the funeral: 'Gott hat
es Betta zuletzt noch gegeben, daß sie erfuhr, was Freundschaft
ist! Ohne Letizia hätte sie viel schlimmer leiden müssen.'(32) The
fisherman Checco's comment is both appropriately conventional
and ironic: 'Letizia ist mehr als tüchtig.'(32) Both approval and
human insight are conveyed by the words of the priest, with
which the story concludes: 'Letizia hat die Beharrlichkeit derer,
die wissen, daß sie auf dem rechten Weg sind.' (33) Saiko's
dialogue has a multi-layered quality; it serves less as commun-
ication between characters than as an externalization of psychological truth.

In *Das andere Leben*, the Mediterranean location serves a rather
different narrative purpose. In *Giraffe unter Palmen* the landscape
stands over against, but simultaneously reflects, the human action;
here, it is the backcloth against which a psychological action
involving two outsiders is developed. A young couple, Harold
and Ellis, are visiting Ellis's elderly aunt who is taking a cure in a
local sanatorium. As they drive to the sanatorium, the road
passes above a bay, the beauty of which makes a powerful impact
on Harold: 'Er deutete mit dem Arm, plötzlich sonderbar
beschwingt, stumm; es war mit Worten wirklich nichts zu sagen.'
(37) There appears to be no road leading down to it. On their
arrival, the autocratic aunt demands that they stay with her at the
sanatorium, but Harold refuses, and sets off alone towards the
bay, while Ellis chooses to stay with the aunt. On arriving at a
secluded village in the bay, Harold looks for somewhere to stay,
but is rebuffed by the villagers – they do not share his idyllic
view of it. The local teacher whom he encounters dismisses his
enthusiasm with contempt: ' "Un paradiso!" . . . "Ein Gefängnis!
. . . Welch primitive und barbarische Art zu leben! Wie kann man

hier bleiben wollen?"' (41) Harold returns to Ellis, who offers a compromise: they will stay not with the aunt, but in a nearby 'Pension'. Harold reflects with bitterness on her betrayal: 'Glaubte sie wirklich, damit den Riß zu verkleben, zu vernebeln, daß sie sich gegen ihn entschieden hatte?' (42) The ending suggests that a turning-point in their relationship has been reached.

The story ostensibly discloses, in a single moment of revelation, the profound incompatibility between the two, the realization of which is triggered off by an apparently trivial event; Harold is powerfully attracted to what he subconsciously needs – absorption into the simple, sensual life of this classical community, where, as he sees it, landscape and people are in harmony – whereas Ellis is concerned only with the material advantages of cultivating the old lady – '. . . eben eine alte Frau, die wir zum Glück einmal beerben werden'. (37) For Harold, the beauty of the landscape is beyond articulation ('es war mit Worten wirklich nichts darüber zu sagen'), whereas Ellis is indifferent to it: '"Ja", nickte Ellis "herrlich! In einer Stunde sind wir bei Tante Celeste".' (37) The critical point of the story is the experience which Harold undergoes after his failed excursion, namely the shock of individuation, hitherto retarded by his failure to achieve, or even seek, a relationship with Ellis that goes deeper than the sexual: at the first moment of tension between them, the thought crosses his mind: 'Ohne Frage wirkte sie in einem ganz physischen Sinn begehrenswert.' (38) The failure of his naïve attempt to enter the peasant world, 'das andere Leben' so romantically perceived, leads directly to his second failure, his alienation from Ellis, which, paradoxically, represents a positive step towards maturation: both the village experience and Ellis herself are in effect a means to that end. The physical location – a self-contained community at the edge of the sea, engaged in a traditional way of life (the cultivation of wine and fruit) – is unidentified. The timeless, sensual qualities of classical myth are imposed upon it by Harold's northern European imagination. Its inaccessibility (to Harold) is symbolically suggested by the 'barrier' of the fishermen's nets, through which he observes the life of the village: 'Er saß vor der Vendita an dem abgescheuerten Tisch, sah durch das Gitterwerk der aufgespannten Netze. Die Frauen stiegen aus den Wein-und Orangengärten herab, flache Bastschüsseln mit Früchten oder Tonkrüge mit Wasser auf den Köpfen balancierend.' (39) Sexual promise is suggested by the yucca tree in front of the church ('. . . ein Yucca von erstaunlicher Höhe, die breite Fächerkrone filigran in den Himmel gestanzt' (39)), as is the description of the young serving girl ('Die Jüngere stellte den Wein und die Trauben vor ihn hin. Sie senkte ihren Blick nicht, sondern nahm den seinen auf, ohne Befangenheit, selbstbewußt, überglänzt von dem, was rings verheißungsvoll aus der im Abend glühenden Bucht hervorbrach' (39)). The story has considerable dramatic and visual power, that 'Prägnanz des Vortrags' characteristic of all these short works,[7] but is trapped in the banality of its characters and situation and fails to create that sense of existential truth suddenly revealed, and that universality of human experience, for which it clearly strives.

Der feindliche Gott, which, exceptionally, is set in North Africa, not in Italy, also takes as its theme the clash of cultures, but narrated here from the point of view of the 'primitive' in its confrontation with a more sophisticated culture. Mabruk, a young Somali tribesman, son of the medicine man, falls into the hands of a European (presumably Italian) military patrol, after escaping into the desert when his village is attacked in a tribal battle. He is taken to the coast and quartered in a barracks, where he undergoes military training. He believes, in accordance with his totemistic religion, that he has now become the property of a new god – the 'killing god' of the foreigners, whom he must serve and propitiate. In this belief, he attempts to acquire skill in the use of the rifle, but fails to master it and is punished. He interprets this failure to mean that his new god demands appeasement through killing, and he shoots dead the colonel of the troops. The story turns on Mabruk's inability to adapt to the mechanistic European values imposed upon him, since his relationship with the external world has been conditioned solely by his animistic beliefs; he must now serve a god whose nature is defined by *Feindlichkeit*, the imperative to kill. Saiko's purpose here is not merely to dramatize the clash of incompatible cultures in the form of a single tragic episode; Mabruk's action is the moment of crisis which abruptly achieves, and at the same time marks the failure of, the process of individuation, which for Mabruk requires his adaptation to the new world of the Europeans. In this process, he endures an extreme of spiritual and emotional, as well as physical, isolation, cut off from the sustaining power of community. Absolute *Einsamkeit* is what links this story with the others,

as Saiko puts it in his commentary: 'Auch in diesem Aufein-
anderprallen zweier grundverschiedener "Merk-und Assozia-
tionswelten" . . . ist der Hauptakkord eines Daseins gegeben, in
dem die Verschmelzung mit dem Du, die Aufhebung der
Einsamkeit immer von neuem scheitern muß.'[8] As in *Giraffe unter
Palmen*, Saiko evokes a sense of the congruence of landscape and
human action. The hostile environment of parched desert and
searing heat externalizes the prevailing culture of death – the
tribal battle and the sphere of the 'killing god'. Language
acquires a particular significance here; Mabruk's failure to orien-
tate himself in his new environment is in part a consequence of
his inability to define correctly, and so internalize, the social organization of the military; his description of the rifle as
'Blitzzauber' or 'der eiserne Stab', the parade-ground orders as
'Schreizauber', the colonel as 'der Älteste', for example, indicate
that he is fatally anchored in a now invalid culture.

Die dunkelste Nacht is effectively a case history of abnormal
psychology. A middle-aged schoolmaster leaves a small Venetian
island to take up a new post in Padua; the ferry journey to the
mainland provides the framework for a series of flashbacks to
recent events – namely the rape and murder of his successor,
Mariarosa, and the theft of her money. Alarmed by the presence
of two *carabinieri* on the boat, he throws the money overboard,
only to discover that their presence is unconnected with his
crime. The point of view of the narrative is vested in the teacher:
he recalls the events and provides insights into his motivation. It
becomes clear that the assault on Mariarosa is the latest in a series
of acts of sexual violence which he has committed, although they
are not described. This incident, however, produces a reaction in
him which is different in kind; he feels a sense of exaltation, that
he has become 'ein anderer als vorher . . . Und endlich – zum
erstenmal – war es nachher nicht "als sei nichts gewesen" wie so
oft.' (53) His recollection of events makes clear that his compulsive violence is the compensation for childhood abuse and
consequent sexual inadequacy. Now, for the first time, he has not
experienced that 'Sturz in das gräßlich mahlende Loch aus Angst
und brennend bitterer Reue' (53) which followed previous
attacks. Responsibility for the assault on Mariarosa is ascribed to his
wife Christina, who has become pregnant and whose habitual
submissiveness, he believes, now masks a determination to force

him to meet his new obligations: 'Ihre Augen hatten plötzlich
etwas Fassungsloses, Ausgeschöpftes, aber dahinter lauerte ein
starrer Entschluß, die Unnachgiebigkeit selbst.' (55) The events of
the story refer exclusively to the sexual sphere – the relationship
with Christina, an encounter with 'die Deutsche' looking for
sexual adventure in Venice, a masked prostitute who takes him to
her room, where he proves to be impotent, and finally Mariarosa.
In this narrative, Saiko again develops his theme of the determining power of the sexual drive over human actions, now in the
extreme form of a pathological compulsion, dramatized by the
compression of a whole life in to a single brief episode and the
deployment of a solipsistic narrator perspective. Here too, however, the focus of the story is the achievement of individuation,
albeit in perverted, destructive form. For the teacher, the
'dunkelste Nacht' is a positive experience; the blackness which
envelops the boat is '. . . schwärzer als alles, was sich ausdenken
ließ' (53) but to him it offers both security and endorsement of his
actions: '. . . er atmete tief, nahm die Nacht in sich hinein wie
etwas Vertrautes – "als habe sie mir tatsächlich geholfen".' (53) If
the night is a sympathetic environment, the city of Venice – the
social domain – is hostile, a stimulus to his paranoia: 'Nur über
Venedig hatte die Nacht nichts vermocht. Venedig war wie der
immerwährende Schrei eines Gottes . . . der Markusplatz stieg
auf und ab im Kampf unsagbarer Kolonnen, die mit schwarzen
und glutroten Speeren übereinander herfielen.' (58) Images of
darkness and light, as signifiers of mental states, recur in the narrative. Saiko also heightens its graphic quality by the use of the
colour blue – the emblem of the remote, the unattainable, the
ideal object of desire – in association with Mariarosa:

> Sie war von Venedig herübergekommen, um nach ihm die Schule
> zu übernehmen. Blau . . . eine gestrickte Jacke, blau ihre Augen –
> wenn die Madonna je einem Sterblichen erschienen war, so nur
> in dieser Gestalt. Nicht annähernd so dünn wie ein Mädchen,
> aber in einer blauen Aura, trotz ihres stumpfschwarzen Haars. (57)

The psychological analysis on which this, and indeed most of
these narratives, is based is familiar terrain: Saiko offers nothing
in the way of new insights, but this story is nevertheless a remarkable projection of intense emotional experience as the
means to self-realization.

Die Statue mit dem Gecko, one of the shortest of the tales, is an account of a chance encounter between a young English couple, Gil and Muriel, and a local youth, on the shore of a small Venetian island. The couple are members of a painting party staying in a local hotel. Gil swims out to sea, leaving Muriel alone. The youth appears suddenly from behind a rock. He is wearing bathing trunks, to which a gecko is attached by a cord. Muriel's initial hostility over this invasion of privacy gives way to fascination, generated by the physical beauty of the youth and the creature itself. He detaches the gecko and transfers it to Muriel's shoulder, securing it to her costume. Gil emerges from the water and the youth disappears. Muriel claims to Gil that she has found the gecko among the rocks. That evening she carries the gecko in public, as she joins her sophisticated friends. The youth is also present, but refuses an invitation to dance with Muriel. She returns the gecko to her room and later discovers that it has disappeared. The story concludes with Muriel's agreement, previously resisted, to Gil's wish to move on the following day. Apart from its overt sexual dynamic, this encounter is significant for the Gil–Muriel relationship in that it articulates the subconscious alienation which already existed unacknowledged – 'als sei eine verborgene Trennungslinie unvermutet sichtbar geworden, eine Entscheidung gefallen'.[9] For Saiko, such sudden moments of self-awareness have existential significance, the emotional shock effects which remind us of the ultimate isolation of individual existence: '. . . fast als bestünde das Leben gerade in seinen entscheidungsvollsten Augenblicken in nichts anderem als in dem Bewußtwerden, daß jeder unentrinnbar seiner Einsamkeit verfallen ist.'[10] Again Saiko projects the interaction between milieu and human experience, the former simultaneously precipitating and reflecting the latter. For Muriel, whose perspective controls the narrative, the island and the sea externalize unfulfilled and, indeed, intellectually unacknowledged, sensual needs: 'Unter ihnen . . . wie wuchernde Flechten in Staub und Sonne, Gemüsegärten, die Zeilen der Weinstöcke und schließlich die Bambuspflanzungen, üppige Grünstreifen zwischen den brandroten Tomatenfeldern.' (73) In a gesture of embrace, 'Muriel breitete die Arme aus'; as she tells Gil, she is 'der Landschaft verfallen'. (73) The instinctive physical gesture and the commonplace phrase mark her surrender to unfamiliar sensual experience, even before the appearance of the youth – and at the same time, her rejection of Gil. At first they swim together 'selig ausgelöscht in Selbstvergessenheit zwischen Himmel und Meer' (73); that *Selbstvergessenheit* involves not only surrender of the self, but also of their relationship. The youth who emerges from the rocks, almost naked, statuesque, the perfect embodiment of sensual beauty and formal proportion, is the archetype of the classical Mediterranean ideal and is immediately recognized as such by Muriel, with her painter's eye: '. . . unwillkürlich suchte sie die Unterteilung der Brust, die ovale Linie der Bauchdecke, die Formen des Kanons'. (75) The transfer of the phallic gecko, both alarming and alluring, symbolizes the replacement of Gil by the youth. At this moment of truth, Gil reappears (because of his long absence Muriel had feared/wished that he had drowned), and the youth vanishes, leaving the gecko behind in Muriel's possession. Muriel's lie about the provenance of the gecko marks the irreversible moment of alienation from Gil – the words make conscious what was hitherto unconscious, and so make it reality. That alienation was already anticipated in the youth's intuitive insight while Gil is still absent: 'Wünschen Sie sich denn im Grunde, daß er nicht zurückkommt?' (75), which he follows with a second question: 'Wozu wollen Sie ihn hier haben? Ihn!' (76) Her attempt to make good the lost opportunity later, in the company of the *Malergesellschaft* in the restaurant, fails: the youth rejects her invitation to dance. The disappearance of the gecko appears to suggest that the moment has been lost for ever, and that she will revert to the routine of the relationship with Gil. However, the critical moment of self-realization has occurred, and cannot be reversed. Her final words indicate that the reconciliation with Gil is provisional: 'Natürlich fahren wir morgen weiter. Ich verstehe sehr gut, daß du nicht hierbleiben willst.' (78) In this story, Saiko continues his theme of culture-clash (*Das andere Leben*, *Der feindliche Gott*) as catalyst in the psychological-emotional process: the collision, here, between the northern European world, represented by the sophisticated, intellectual, but fatigued and sexually repressed *Malergesellschaft*, and the instinctive, sensual *heile Welt* of the Mediterranean – between the relativism of the one and the absolute of the other. The youth has a clearer sense of this opposition than Muriel; the direct expression of sexual desire is natural in his world, not in hers – hence his rejection of her advances. In his integration of landscape and human experience, Saiko employs sensual images of heat, light and beauty to create a powerful, even mythic, sense of place, but also to serve as a correlative to the psychological action. Direct speech, although minimal, has significant psychological resonance. For example, the youth's first statement to Muriel, 'Es ist meine Badestelle . . . Ich kann gehen, wenn Sie es wünschen' (74), is, on the surface, a harmless remark – a simple assertion of his proprietorial rights and a polite concession to a stranger – but it also articulates Muriel's suppressed desires. 'Wenn Sie es wünschen' brings into the conscious sphere the tension which will determine both present and future; she does *not* wish it, nor is it even in her power to wish it. His subsequent questions are those she will now put to herself – 'Wünschen Sie sich denn im Grunde, daß er nicht zurückkommt?' and 'Wozu wollen Sie ihn hier haben?': the conscious realization of the unconscious. This is Saiko's 'magischer Realismus' in action, in which the 'Agens der Tiefe', the well-springs of the subconscious, break through to the surface.[11] For Muriel, the past is now finished; when Gil returns, he responds to her claim to have found the gecko among the rocks with the bitter comment: 'Mitten im Schreck über mein Verschwinden? . . . Also eine Art Ablenkung?' Muriel replies 'Genau das!' (77): the speech act opens up the emotional abyss which can never again be closed.

Die Geburt des Lammes, an equally short text, also involves northern Europeans in a Mediterranean setting. It also turns on a crisis in a relationship which brings about a permanent break in that relationship which implies a new beginning, and foregrounds the woman's experience. Gerda and Paul, members of a touring party, visit a pagan fertility temple, now overrun with grazing sheep. On all sides, birth is taking place – a mare by the roadside, watched by a pregnant woman, a ewe within the temple perimeter. Gerda herself is pregnant, although Paul is unaware of the fact. The dialogue reveals that Paul has insisted that they should not have a child, for reasons that involve self-interest, but also derive from his rational-aesthetic temperament, which keeps life at a distance. His comment on the temple is indicative: 'Man sieht es wieder, Architektur ist eben doch hauptsächlich Proportion.' (82) Gerda believes in the rightness of her decision for motherhood; as they observe the ewe's birth pangs, Gerda turns bitterly on Paul with: 'Du solltest sie zu Herbert auf die Klinik schicken', a reference, it would appear, to a friend who carries out abortions. Paul replies: 'Natürlich, ich würde dich ihm mit gutem Gewissen anvertrauen!', to which Gerda replies: 'Ach ja, dein gutes Gewissen! – nach meinem wird nicht gefragt.' (83) Gerda, aware of the pact they had made earlier, and anticipating his violent reaction, does not disclose her condition to Paul. Yet the decisive break between them has been made, though not yet put into words: 'Plötzlich war Paul ein fremder Mann.' (84) The ewe gives birth, Gerda approaches the animal, but is warned off by the ram guarding her and she sarcastically compares Paul with the protective ram. As they cross the narrow, exposed path leading into the temple interior, Gerda feels a powerful compulsion to push Paul off the path to his possible death. The moment passes, leaving Gerda in a state of shock. Rejoining the company in the tavern, Gerda provokes Paul by offering to accompany one of the men back to the temple. The implication is that the relationship with Paul is over and that Gerda may be about to embark on a new one. Her friend Susanna comforts Gerda, stating her belief that what matters is always 'sich von neuem entschließen zu können', but the story concludes with Gerda in tears, as she confronts the dead past – 'Gerdas vom Weinen zuckender Mund hatte keine Entgegnung'. (86) The narrative is littered with images of fertility – not merely in the multiple references to birth, both animal and human, but in the insistent symbolism of the landscape itself: 'In der Talsenke verschwand das Flüßchen in einem quellend-grünen Tümpel, durchwuchert von Sumpfgras, Schilf und dichtgefiederten Bamusstangen: der üppige Nabel lebendiger Fruchtbarkeit . . . ' (81) Here nature replicates the female sexual organ, and the temple itself is womb-like, accessible only by the narrow passage on which Paul so nearly meets his death because he has forfeited his right to participate in the act of procreation. For Gerda the process of individuation, as her 'dunkelste(n) Selbstverlorenheit an ihn' gives way to 'ein sehnsüchtiges Vorgefühl des Eigentlichen' (84), can only be realized by the 'elimination' of Paul, whose denial of the principle of life is a sacrilege against the 'Fruchtbarkeitsgöttin' of the temple. The story succeeds in conveying something of the intensity of the woman's experience and the critical workings of the subconscious, but suffers from its symbolic overload and narrative contrivance.

Hafen der Venus reworks a number of the ideas and motifs already encountered in the collection. A couple travelling in the south become involved in a triangular situation, which brings to the surface the true nature of their relationship, leads to a crisis and ultimately to an ambiguous reconciliation. Alfred and Therese are on their honeymoon in a hotel on the coast. They observe the behaviour of some fellow guests – an Italian family group of husband, wife and child. The brutality of the husband's treatment of wife and son provokes a sexual response in Therese. Alfred, many years her senior and jealous, senses the truth and proposes that they move on elsewhere. Therese attempts to attract the man, but her flirtatious approaches are contemptuously dismissed. As she goes up to her room, however, he follows and forces himself upon her, although Therese is a willing, if passive, victim. Throughout the episode she fails to maintain the attitude of detachment which she had, as it were, 'rehearsed' in her imagination, and so finds herself playing out the submissive role of the man's wife, of which she had initially expressed (in part, as provocation) theoretical approval to Alfred: 'Ah – leben wir nicht viel zu sehr in der Vernunft und Rücksicht, in den Konventionen? . . . also aus den Gründen der Hygiene!' (90) Following the encounter, Therese turns back to Alfred – 'Du weißt doch, wie nötig ich dich habe' (96) – and so endorses the 'Vernunft', 'Rücksicht' and 'Konventionen' she had earlier rejected. Alfred allows himself to be reassured, since he fears her loss. *Hafen der Venus* is less transparent in its psychology than the stories discussed above. It does not define an irreversible moment of emotional transition in the central figure, but suggests a more problematic confrontation between ego and subconscious, which is finally unresolved – that is to say, the desire for control over self is in conflict with the desire to abandon that control in instinctive action. The narrative strategy is also interesting here: Therese, as narrator, effectively controls her own story, but the experience she narrates involves a progressive loss of control, which creates an ironic tension between fable and narration which is unique in this collection. The catalyst for the psychological action is again suggested emblematically by the cultural collision of North and South – the sophisticated, rational sphere and that of instinctive action. The glass door set in the corridor to Therese's room provides the most striking image in the narrative;

Therese senses that the Italian is following her, and closes and locks the glass door between them, but then presses her body and lips against it, in a gesture at once defensive and inviting – 'War die Glastür nicht herrlich, hinter der sie endlich ihre deutlichste Sprache fand! Und sie, Therese selbst, würde diese Tür zertrümmern.' (94) This ambivalence of action is indeed 'ihre deutlichste Sprache'.

Das offene Tor, the final and by far the longest of the stories, is also the most difficult, not least at the basic level of comprehensibility. It is set in an obscure quarter of Venice, and opens with the discovery by Donna Rosetta and her wedding guests of the body of her bridegroom, Rinuccio Mielli, hanging in a grocer's shop undergoing reconstruction. The narrative retraces the development of the Rosetta–Rinuccio relationship. Rinuccio, a public archivist, first visits Rosetta in connection with some papers left by her husband. They become lovers, but the affair is complicated by the interference of a sometime suitor of Rosetta, Serafino, known as 'Der Kapitän', and described as 'ein Freund des Hauses' and, additionally, by an affair between Rinuccio and Gelsonima, who is (possibly) Rosetta's niece. Serafino threatens Rinuccio with exposure to the police (since Gelsomina is under age) unless he marries Rosetta. The suggestion is also made that Rinuccio's relationship with his mother had been incestuous. The narrator throws no clear light on the motive for Rinuccio's suicide, and the reader is left with the (probably unreliable) speculations of various members of the wedding party; Rosetta blames it on Serafino's handling of the Gelsonima affair, Serafino on Rinuccio's late realization that he would be marrying beneath him, Clementina on Rinuccio's mother's disapproval from beyond the grave. The story concludes with Rosetta's invitation to Serafino to accompany her home – presumably as a ready replacement for Rinuccio. *Das offene Tor* has something in common with *Die dunkelste Nacht* in its account of abnormal psychology, as well as its Venetian background, but lacks its narrative focus – the absence of a clear narrator standpoint, either external or internal to the story, means that dialogue and thought sequences, for example, are often unattributable. The obscurity of the narrative line is, of course, also an occasional feature of Saiko's novels. In this story, where he attempts to paint a broader social, and a more diverse psychological, canvas than in the shorter works, the writing is less disciplined. The structure of the story, opening with the shocking event of the suicide and returning by means of a series of flashbacks to that event, would seem to suggest that Saiko's intention is to throw light on the psychological factors contributing to the suicide. Little light emerges. Where the story works well, however, is in its account of the sturdy resilience of the small community of characters, in whose lives Rinuccio has become involved. Death, however grotesque its form, is an unremarkable fact of existence and is dealt with with unsentimental robustness. Rinuccio is dead, so belongs to the past, and Rosetta moves on to fill the gap by accepting Serafino. Through the eyes of the witnesses, Rinuccio has now become no more than 'ein Paket getrockneter Stockfische', 'das schlotterige Bündel', 'das längliche Bündel'. Their shared emotion is not one of grief but of 'Erbitterung' – their plans have been frustrated.

In his *Erinnerungen an einen fast Unbekannten*,[12] Kurt Benesch recalls a casual reference to his Mediterranean stories made by Saiko (to 'ein paar Bekannte(n) im Café Glory hinter der Votivkirche') – 'Ich hab da so ein paar erotische Geschichten . . . Aber die nimmt ja niemand.'[13] The grounds for Saiko's pessimism doubtless lay in part in his difficult experiences at the hands of publishers, in Austria and elsewhere, starting with his struggles to bring out *Auf dem Floß*,[14] but also in part in his awareness that his work would achieve little, or no, popular resonance. It is a constant of the creative period of Saiko's life that he sought a wider readership – not least for economic reasons – but could not make the artistic compromises which might achieve that end. As his essay on these short stories, referred to above, makes clear, however, he had no doubts about the quality of his work nor the significance of its contribution to Austrian, and European, literary culture.

These stories stand apart from Saiko's major works, in that they were written, or at least conceived, 'on vacation' (although this is not to suggest that they are in any sense casual pieces – they are as meticulously crafted as anything he wrote). That is to say, they do not bear, even indirectly, on the Austrian *Problematik* with which the larger works are exclusively concerned, that 'Thematisierung des Österreichischen', as Haslinger puts it,[15] with which Saiko was preoccupied in the post-war period. It may be that the Mediterranean world, so attractive to Saiko, represented an escape from the material rigours of life in the decade after 1945, and also from his deep concern over the current political and ideological situation in Austria and his despair as to its future direction (trenchantly summarized in his essay *Hinter dem Gesicht des Österreichers* of 1957[16]). If the setting of these stories is exotic, the psychological positions which underlie them are unchanged; here, too, the key themes are the interaction of external situation or event and individual psychology, the compulsive nature of the sexual drive and the moment of self-realization by means of which the 'Stachel der Bedrohung' of the dark and destructive forces of the subconscious can be neutralized. The Mediterranean world, however, is represented less as a social reality than as a construct of archetypes, symbols and mythic powers, which releases or stimulates psychological activity. At their best, these stories brilliantly illustrate the distinctive qualities of Saiko's narrative style – linguistic precision, extreme compression, economy of means, significant dialogue and striking visual imagery. They make demands on the reader and reward the effort.

Notes

Textual references are to *George Saiko. Erzählungen* (Zurich–Cologne, 1972).

[1] Those contemporary writers include Hermann Broch, Franz Theodor Csokor, Felix Braun, Heimito von Doderer and Jeannie Ebner.

[2] See, for example, the recent substantial collection of essays *George Saikos magischer Realismus*, ed. Joseph Strelka (Bern, 1990), with its subtitle 'Zum Werk eines unbekannten großen Autors'.

[3] As far as I am aware no exclusive study of the *Giraffe unter Palmen* collection has appeared as yet.

[4] In George Saiko, 'Zur Entschlüsselung der Symbolik in zwei Kurzgeschichten', in *Literatur und Kritik*, 14 (1967), 214. Note that Saiko refers to himself in the third person in this essay.

[5] Ibid.

[6] Ibid.

[7] Ibid.

[8] Ibid., 215.

9 Ibid.

10 Ibid.

11 See Saiko's discussion of 'magischer Realismus' in his essay 'Der Roman – Heute und Morgen', in *Wort in der Zeit*, 9 (1963).

12 Reprinted in *George Saiko. Sämtliche Werke in fünf Bänden*, vol. 5 (Salzburg/Vienna, 1985–9), pp. 329–36.

13 Ibid., p. 334.

14 See, for example, the Broch–Saiko correspondence, in *George Saiko. Sämtliche Werke in fünf Bänden*, vol. 5, *passim*.

15 Ibid., p. 363.

16 Ibid., vol. 4, pp. 203–15.

7

Eine sagenhafte Figur (1946) – An Allegorical Novel of the Status Quo. The Re-emergence of Albert Paris Gütersloh at the end of the Second World War

JÖRG THUNECKE

The date 16 August 1940 was a decisive day in the artistic career of Albert Paris Gütersloh (1887–1973);[1] for it was on this day that the president of the 'Reichskammer der bildenden Künste' in Berlin issued a decree amounting to a *Berufsverbot* for Gütersloh, covering the whole of the German Reich.[2] In fact, the letter announcing this decision arrived in the wake of Gütersloh's dismissal (*Amtsenthebung*) as professor at the 'Staatliche Kunstgewerbeschule' (Academy of Applied Arts) in Vienna in 1938, shortly after the *Anschluß*,[3] and led to the subsequent cancellation of his membership of the 'Gesellschaft bildender Künstler Wiens (Künstlerhaus)',[4] stating:

> Auf Grund der Überprüfung aller Voraussetzungen für Ihre Kammerzugehörigkeit besitzen Sie nach den in Ihren persönlichen Verhältnissen begründeten Tatsachen nicht die erforderliche Zuverlässigkeit, um an der Förderung deutscher Kultur in Verantwaltung gegenüber Volk und Reich mitzuwirken. Sie erfüllen mithin nicht die Voraussetzungen für die Mitgliedschaft bei der Reichskammer der bildenden Künste. Gemäß dem §10 der Ersten Durchführungsverordnung zum Reichskulturkammergesetz vom 1.11.33 (RGBl. I, S.797) lehne ich Ihre Aufnahme in die Reichskammer der bildenden Künste ab und untersage Ihnen mit sofortiger Wirkung jede berufliche – auch nebenberufliche – Betätigung auf den Gebieten der bildenden Künste.

Ultimately, Gütersloh was not merely prohibited from pursuing a career as a painter, but was effectively barred from any artistic engagement – even as a writer – during the war years, and eventually forced to work (*Zwangsverpflichtung*) as a clerk in an aeroplane factory at Fischamend, near today's Schwechat International Airport.[5] Not until the liberation of Austria by Allied forces, in April 1945, was he able officially to resume his activities as a writer and painter.

Gütersloh had originally made his mark as a writer with a highly acclaimed Expressionist novel, *Die tanzende Törin* (1910), followed in the 1920s, in quick succession, by another four volumes, two of them also novels, *Innozenz oder Sinn und Fluch der Unschuld* and *Der Lügner unter Bürgern* (both 1922).[6] Despite playing a highly influential role in Austrian culture during the inter-war years, Gütersloh's reputation and position then, as today, 'is hardly reflected in his reception by the general public', and '[h]is highly complex, intricately sophisticated, difficult, and often extremely abstract novels found only a small audience among readers'.[7] This may explain why the Viennese publisher Rudolf Haybach, who stuck with Gütersloh until 1930 (the publication of Doderer's *Der Fall Gütersloh*), having published two other books of his,[8] eventually gave up when it came to placing Gütersloh's latest novel, *Eine sagenhafte Figur*.[9] Gütersloh had started this novel in 1927, and completed it, up to a point, in mid-1930.[10] As a result, this novel was not published until after the Second World War, followed by *Die Fabeln vom Eros* (1947), *Sonne und Mond* (1962), *Der Innere Erdteil* (1966), and *Die Fabel von der Freundschaft* (1969), heralding the re-emergence of Gütersloh as a writer of some reputation which has lasted into our time.[11]

Tension between truth and untruth dominates Gütersloh's œuvre,[12] beginning with the upper-middle-class novel *Die tanzende Törin*, continuing in the lower-middle-class milieu of *Der Lügner unter Bürgern*, and persisting right through to his *opus magnum*, *Sonne und Mond* (1962). Nowhere is Gütersloh's indefatigable search for truth, the individual's effort to come to terms with himself, more pronounced, however, than in *Eine sagenhafte Figur*, characteristically subtitled 'Ein platonischer Roman'. Though Platonic ideas – apart from the key issue of the search for truth – are *not* at the heart of this novel, the link with Plato, to which the subtitle refers, none the less exists, hinging on the dialogic structure of this work, as pointed out by Felix Thurner in his study on Gütersloh:

> Ohne philosophische Hintergründigkeit wird die Verbindung zu Platon klar, wenn man in dessen Dialogwerk die aesthetischen Bauformen berücksichtigt. Gütersloh meint mit seinem Hinweis die platonische Art des Vortrags, nicht platonische Lehrmeinungen.[13]

Although *Eine sagenhafte Figur* employs a first-person narrator, operating within a fictional framework, only in the appended afterword[14] is he given genuine authorial status, while over large sections of the narrative the impression is gained that the hero of the novel, the aristocrat Kirill Ostrog, primarily speaks *pro domo*, echoing the author, and that only his conversations with various fictional characters about fundamental moral issues really matter. In fact, *Eine sagenhafte Figur* is Gütersloh's novel of an idealist, in which the author 'treibt das bohrende Fragen des Helden bis zur . . . moralischen Entscheidung.'[15]

Gütersloh's novels, particularly the ones published after World War II, have invariably been described as 'unzeitgemäß', 'antimodern', and 'traditionalistisch',[16] labels which no doubt also apply to *Eine sagenhafte Figur*. So, while the individual's search for inner renewal is an essential ingredient of the wider-ranging 'geistig-sittlichen Erneuerung'[17] Gütersloh aimed for in his fiction, the narrative approach equally reflects his 'Kampf gegen den Belletrismus' (Doderer), his rejection of the inclusion of fictional details for the reader's sake, and his advocacy of a kind of 'Entschlackung des Inhalts', 'ein Schreiben ohne Leser, . . . das nicht auf das Publikum und dessen Unterhaltung blickt . . . '[18]

Consequently, none of Gütersloh's novels is particularly content-orientated. It is not realistic detail that is of prime importance but dialectical thought processes (usually expressed in tense dialogic exchanges), and as a result the author – though far from aiming at writing historical novels – often based his plots in times of historical upheavals, and at points of socio-political watersheds (like Hebbel in his plays more than three-quarters of a century earlier), identified by one critic as the era immediately preceding the 'Untergang Kakaniens',[19] that is, the last years of the reign of Emperor Francis Joseph.[20]

In *Eine sagenhafte Figur*, more than in any other of his novels, Gütersloh used the historical events leading up to the outbreak of the First World War as a catalyst for the solution of his hero's personal problems. In other words, what matters primarily is not the historical situation but the ideological consequences of these events: 'Fruchtbar wird bei ihm die geistige Wende, der Punkt der ideengeschichtlichen Umwälzung. Ihm signalisiert die Zeit den Aufbruch neuer Ideen und folgenreicher gesellschaftlicher Umschichtungen.'[21]

The plot of the 484-page novel runs roughly as follows:[22]

Kirill Ostrog, a man in his early twenties, of aristocratic background, and fostered since childhood by a highly respectable middle-class family (a professor, his wife, and their two daughters, Laura and Bettina), comes of age. The narrative begins with the foster-father's decision to give a surprise engagement party for Kirill and Laura. In ignorance of Laura's rejection of an earlier proposal by Kirill, a well-guarded secret for two years, the foster-parents and all the guests think of the two young people as lovers. As a result of the refusal by the betrothed to reveal the truth, the unsavoury situation is institutionalized. However, the repression of the truth also leads to Laura being partially paralysed. A physician tells Kirill that Laura's illness is caused by a hysterical condition, brought about by her fear of incest, having all her life thought of Kirill as a brother rather than as a lover. The physician recommends that Kirill should use the outbreak of the Great War as a solution for his personal problems. When Kirill announces his decision to enlist as a soldier, his foster-father informs him how the warmongers in the Cabinet dragged the country into this fateful encounter, and how he was offered the job as Minister of the Interior, which he rejected. He vents his anger at Kirill's decision; Laura, on the other hand, now falls in love with the man willing to sacrifice his life for his country. The draft board, however, finds Kirill unfit for military service. Suspecting that his foster-father influenced this decision, Kirill, all adrift, pays a visit to a high-class brothel run by a fellow aristocrat, and falls in love with a whore called Tamila. Despite their mutual feeling for each other, Kirill, after a night's love-making, thinks that his obligations towards Laura must prevail over his feelings for Tamila, leaving her in the full knowledge of having missed a unique opportunity to lead a fulfilled life. In a somewhat disjointed afterword, written and appended by the author to the main text of the novel after the Second World War, friends of the protagonist coincidentally meet Kirill in Cagnes-sur-mer on the French Riviera, where he leads a withdrawn life as a painter, brooding about the past, and deluding himself about the present.

As pointed out by more than one critic, summarizing the plot of Gütersloh's novel in this way creates a false impression; for, as Thurner noted: 'Auch hier lag es dem Autor fern, einen gradlinigen Liebesroman oder einen Gesellschaftsroman im üblichen Sinne zu schreiben.'[23]

The real issue of this novel, succinctly put by Ludwig Fischer, and discussed at length below, is the theme that '[t]he tenacious clinging to outdated meaningless traditions brings frustration and creates a world of illusion and lies for [the] protagonist, but also . . . security, which, when abandoned, and when living at risk outside the old structures, turns into dangerous all-destroying chaos'.[24]

As mentioned earlier, the plot of *Eine sagenhafte Figur* centres on the days immediately before and after the outbreak of the First World War at the end of July and the beginning of August 1914. However, as also emphasized previously, Gütersloh used the war merely as a catalyst to focus on the personal problems of his protagonist. 'Der Krieg da draußen und der Krieg hier drinnen treffen nicht zufällig zusammen', Kirill admits in an attempt to justify himself before his foster-father: 'Vielmehr ist der eine nur die Fortsetzung des andern . . .',[25] a statement showing profound insight into the link between the decadence of state and society in the Austro-Hungarian Empire in 1914. As a member of the ruling class ('Kaste' is the term used (86)) – despite having been brought up as a bourgeois – Kirill is keenly aware of living in a state rotten through and through ('in einem großen Spital' (103)), and that he is part of a society which has chosen to ignore the gulf between those who, metaphorically speaking, live 'zu ebner

Erde' (20), 'die gerechte, die gesunde, die nicht krankhaft ver-
zerrte Welt' (43), and those 'im ersten Stock' (20), 'von wirklicher
Liebe so weit entfernt wie von der wahren Wahrheit und von
dem echten Drange nach dem echten Leben'. (42) None the less,
as intimated by the narrator near the beginning of the novel, at
no point of the narrative is Kirill able, or even genuinely willing,
to break with what he recognizes to be a 'lebensmüdes Geschlecht' and an 'entnervter Staat' (250):

> Mit dem tausendarmigen Labyrinth der Zärtlichkeiten und
> Rücksichten, mit seinen abertausend heimlichen Opfergängen zu
> den Altären des *Alten und Bewährten*, mit den unendlich vielen . .
> . Überwindungen unseres eigenen Willens hat das Familienleben
> uns ausgehöhlt. Wir können also den geraden Weg gar nicht
> mehr gehen [*my italics*]. (20–1)[26]

Consequently, by setting out to illustrate that the protagonist of
Eine sagenhafte Figur is a 'Liebhaber des Alten' and 'eiserner Ritter
des Gestern' (434), who only knows one enemy – change[27] –
Gütersloh, in effect, wrote a novel which, in allegorical disguise,
attacks the status quo of the political and social structure of the
Austro-Hungarian Empire on the eve of the First World War. In a
series of dialogic exchanges, some of them in the form of confes-
sions – prompting one critic to call *Eine sagenhafte Figur* a 'Buch
der Beichten'[28] – with men and women from different walks of
life, Kirill's idealism, undeniably founded on high moral principles, is exposed as misguided and untenable. The author, in
fact, portrays his hero as 'einer jener fast schon ausgestorbener
Menschen, die ihr Gesetz mit sich führen' (380), a legendary
figure ('sagenhafte Figur' (383, 386)), painting him as a kind of
dinosaur on the verge of extinction, whose personal situation
resembles that of the country at large in the summer of 1914,
'unmittelbar vor dem Zusammenbruch seiner politischen und
seiner geographischen Einheit'. (171)

The dialogic exchanges[29] are all the result of Kirill's chance encounters with people outside his own sphere, offering different
social perspectives, and invariably leading to, and concentrating
on, the question of dishonesty in his relationship with his supposed fiancée: two of these exchanges take the form of 'confes-
sions', though the 'advice' of the confessor is rejected in each

instance; another two are verbal confrontations with his foster-sister Bettina, and with a young army volunteer, and can be regarded as successful manœuvres by the protagonist to discuss, and in a sense off-load, some of the very problems he himself refuses to address; in the remaining two dialogues the hero faces the challenge (*Unterweisung* (350)) of a vagabond, and finds himself engaged in a rearguard action fending off a whore who has fallen in love with him.

The protagonist's first 'confession' (*Beichte* (71)) takes place in one of the capital's public gardens, where he sought refuge after a night agonizing over a solution for the hypocritical relationship with his foster-sister. The chance meeting with a militant young socialist offers him an opportunity to review his role in society, having informed the stranger of his recent resolve to terminate his engagement: for after two years of lying about the true nature of his liaison with Laura (70), to protect his fiancée's honour (79), and to secure their position in society, he has decided 'der . . . Braut die Freiheit und mir . . . das Los der Verbannung zu werfen'. (69) In reply to the socialist's query as to why he is asking the advice of a total stranger, who also happens to be a class enemy ('ein Feind dieser ihrer Klasse' (73)), Kirill offers a revealing insight into the decadent and mendacious life-style of the Austrian ruling classes of his day, solely concerned with safeguarding their own interests. In fact, he feels compelled to admit that to be judged fairly for his failures would require ruthless peers, capable, 'nicht nur mich zu verurteilen . . . , sondern auch meine ganze Welt, welche zugleich die ihre ist, also auch sich selbst. . . ' (71–2), whereas it seems almost certain,

> daß ich freigesprochen würde, und zwar unter dem unwiderstehlichen Drucke unseres Axiom gewordenen Glaubens, die mein . . . Empfinden und Handeln bestimmenden Umstände seien die ewig selben, allüberall mit der Gültigkeit eines Gesetzes der Physik auftretenden der ganzen Menschheit, und nicht . . . die von überlang geübter Inzucht innerhalb einer begrenzten Klasse hervorgebrachten zweiten Wirklichkeit. (72)

Despite such revelations about the decadence of his own class, Kirill cannot be persuaded to abandon his current life-style,

preferring self-delusion ('Zustand der frommen Täuschung' (81))
to a lifeline offered him by the socialist: 'Also auf, . . . stürzen Sie
sich ins Meer, und erreichen Sie glücklich die Küste, wo die neuen
Menschenfischer wohnen' (83), insisting that old-fashioned dignity
and inherited loyalties must prevail:

> Wie Greise die Wärme des Ofens hüten, so hütet das absterbende
> Geschlecht unter dem schönen Vorwand von *Würde und Treue* die
> Türen und Fugen zur ringsum aufsteigenden neuen Zeit, damit
> kein Hauch des neuen Frühlings den *Vorgang des Zerfalls* störe
> und den unvermeidlichen *Tod des Alten* noch bitterer mache [*my
> italics*]. (85)

And in the end, contrary to the socialist's suggestion ('lassen Sie
die Toten ihre Toten begraben' (84)), yet as a direct result of it,
Kirill feels strongly reminded of his class obligations, sensing
that he had been on the verge of betraying his own people: 'ich
übte fast Verrat an den Meinen, . . . und habe durch Sie erst meine
Pflicht erkannt.' (87)

The bulk of Kirill's conversation with the family doctor, the
second of six dialogic exchanges in *Eine sagenhafte Figur*, is
devoted to an explanation of Laura's medical condition. In connection with the search for a possible cure for her illness, which
the physician – fully conversant with recent advances in the field
of psychoanalysis[30] – treats as an affliction rather than a serious
disease (he refers to 'die seelischen Ursachen des nur scheinbar
körperlichen Leidens' (101)), he appeals to the baron's conscience
to inform him truthfully of all the accompanying circumstances.
As a result, Kirill is persuaded to admit to having been turned
down by Laura two years before, and to confess details of the
engaged couple's tacit agreement. (104) At the same time though,
he once again rejects any suggestion of budging from his position
of leaving the household of his adopted parents, by now a *cause
d'honneur*, rather than cancelling the engagement. Indeed, in
rebuffing the doctor, he pointedly refers to an earlier rejection of
proposals made by the socialist to change his life-style:

> Ähnlich wie jenem, antworte ich auch Ihnen: ich bleibe in meiner
> Krankheit, ich stehe still bei meiner Schuld wie die Ehrenwache
> beim fürstlichen Katafalk. Nicht alle . . . fliehen, wenn der Vulkan
> ausbricht. Nicht wenige bleiben in dem Vaterhause an der
> lebenden Flanke des Berges. In ihnen lebt noch *der alte Sinn*, der

überall sonst schon abhanden gekommen ist oder eben aus-
gerottet wird [*my italics*]. (103–4)

Following such a statement of principles, no amount of goading
and exhortation can persuade Kirill to abandon his adopted
stance: neither the charge of hypocrisy, boasting of being an
Ordnungsmann while failing in his everyday duties ('Pflichten im
kleinen' (118)), nor the insult of being called an idealistic fool
('idealistischer Tropf' (121)), who is trying to escape into hollow
ideals ('die Weite der hallenden Ideale' (119)) rather than offer
sexual fulfilment to a fiancée, portrayed by the doctor as a lech-
erous young girl ('ein wollüstiges Mädchen' (121)). On the contrary, despite the doctor's admonition, Kirill firmly believes that
he will soon return to the status quo of his previous routine:
'Noch so sehr willens, fremdem Geisteslicht zu folgen,' he con-
cedes, 'wird der Mensch unter dem Druck der eigenen ['sagenhafte[n]'/JT] Figur . . . bald wieder die nur ihm gemäßen Kreise
ziehen' (122–3); and he is therefore only too happy to grasp a
straw offered him by the physician: 'Vielleicht löst an Ihrer Stelle
der Krieg das heikle Problem. Sie fallen auf dem Feld der Ehre . . .'
(123)

Kirill's verbal clashes with his foster-sister Bettina, and at a
later stage with a young army volunteer, are both the result of an
inability to come to terms with his own personal problems, and
an attempt to distract from them by interfering with somebody
else's: 'Mit nichts als mit mir beschäftigt, änderte ich ein fremdes
Leben' (234), he admits. In fact, both encounters bring about a
vital change in the life of the antagonist, while the protagonist
continues to cling rigidly to the status quo of his current existence: 'grimmig darauf aus, über einen andren zu entscheiden,
weil ich über mich nicht entscheiden konnte.' (219)

In the case of Bettina, Kirill accuses his foster-sister of being
too servile and frigid, suppressing all personal inclinations, and
advises her to join a nunnery, ignoring (repressing?) the fact that
only a short while ago the physician had entreated him to be
more worldly (less of a 'strahlende[r] Gott') and more open
towards Laura's sexual problems ('ein[em] lustgequälte[n]
arme[n] Menschen' (114)):[31]

Der Sehnsuchtsschmerz, der mich zur einen bog, schleuderte den
Pfeil auf die andre. Weil ich das blutunterlaufene Zentrum

meines männlichen Ziels vor Augen hatte, traf ich so grausam ins Schwarze eines nonnenhaften Wesens. (241)

Similarly, Kirill's efforts in dissuading a young volunteer from enlisting in the imperial army are a way of deliberately distracting from his own personal failings: 'Hier stand ich,' he confesses, 'ein verfehltes Leben zu beginnen, oder ein sehr sinnvolles sinnlos zu enden.' (257–8) Far from telling the truth that his own decision to enlist is guided by fate ('Schicksal'), and that of his fellow volunteer by cool calculation ('Überlegung'),[32] it soon emerges that Kirill contemplates suicide ('den Tod für die Bagatelle meines Lebens' (270)) and is trying to accomplish a role-reversal:[33] the decadent and guilt-ridden nobleman, who openly defied his foster-father not to join the army as a volunteer, actively encourages his pure and innocent bourgeois counterpart to boycott his late father's wish to become a soldier. Though the young volunteer senses that something is wrong with their respective positions ('Vielleicht verfehlen Sie den Sinn, den Sie hier suchen und erfüllen einen, den Sie nicht suchen' (276)), Kirill's justification of the double life led by the volunteer's father (that is, the dilemma, 'daß man in Lagen kommen kann, die uns eine Wahrheit erkennen lassen, aber zugleich den erlösenden Gebrauch dieser Wahrheit verbieten' (286)), convinces the young man that he misunderstood his father, that he must alter his plans for the future, and abandon the status quo of his current life-style, a decision far more appropriate if it had been taken by Kirill himself. 'Mein Gott!', the young man exclaims at this turn of events, 'sind Sie denn heute gekommen, nicht nur das Gegenwärtige zu zerstören, sondern bis in meine frühe Jugend Ihr grausames klares Licht zu ergießen . . .?' (287) Kirill actually feels more like a missionary at this stage ('Hier war wieder einer – Bettina gedachte ich da! – den ich aufs Pferd gesetzt habe, daß er weite Sicht hätte . . .' (307)), having succeeded in crushing the young man's patriotic enthusiasm and persuading him to become a conscientious objector.[34] 'Die nicht auf Ihren hohen Stufen stehen,' Kirill exhorts him, 'dürfen glauben das Vaterland zu verteidigen. Sie aber müssen wissen, daß Sie nur töten und dürfen hinter patriotischem Vorwand nicht Verzeihung für ein Verbrechen suchen . . .', continuing:

Sie . . . wird schon bei dem ersten Schusse die rettende Vorstellung verlassen, ihn fürs enge Vaterland und gegen die weite
feindliche Welt abgegeben zu haben. Sie werden den Bruder
sehn, und vergeblich den Mördergleichmut suchen bei den
Ideenbildern der Pflicht. (308)

Equally revealing is Kirill's encounter with a vagabond on a
highway leading out of the capital, shortly after his rejection by
the draft board. The tramp immediately senses that his com-
panion is no more than a mere 'Amateur[ ] des Unglücks' and
'Stümper der Zerstörung' (344), one of those idealists who
believe that 'der Bruch mit dem Alten und der Sprung ins Neue,
sie machten sich von selber, einfach aus den unleidlichen
Umständen!' (344) Consequently, he argues that men like Kirill,
likely to incur social decline if they relinquish the status quo of
their current position,[35] merely fool themselves by trying to turn
over a new leaf ('wer was zu verlassen hat, der verläßt es nicht!'
(344)). He effectively destroys Kirill's hopes of 'starting a new life'
('Anfang eines neuen Lebens' (345)) – if necessary by means of
role reversal or transfer[36] – by exposing it as an empty phrase,
used by the upper echelons of society to justify their existence,
and scornfully rejected by the vagabond as 'eines der vielen
hohlen Worte aus eurem Sprachschatz, aus der Großbank eures
Gehirns, die alle Begriffe aufgekauft hat, wie euer Staat alles
Gold . . . Aber ein Windpfiff durch ein Spundloch hat mehr Sub-
stanz.' (348)

If earlier encounters with the socialist and the physician had
offered Kirill the chance of leading either a working-class life or
that of a married man, the confrontation with the vagabond takes
him to a crossroads, which before long becomes a road of no
return; for when he meets and falls in love with Tamila at the bor-
dello of his aristocratic friend Ottokar, he is at last forced to make
a choice between love and duty: 'das bescheidene, aber dauernde
Glück der Sinne', or 'd[ie] dauernde[] Unruhe eines nur unglück-
lich sich glücklich fühlenden Geistes'. (367)

A decision in favour of Tamila, sacrificing his principles on the
altar of love ('Wenn ich mit dem Herzen auch das Gewissen ver-
löre' (373)), would have gained Kirill what he had craved for and
been denied by Laura during the past two years. However, contrary to his earlier, mendacious justification of the double life of

the volunteer's father, sensing an 'Empfindung der Auflösung' (373), he now claims that one cannot love two women at the same time without being untrue to oneself; and seeing no alternative, he opts for a 'besinnungslose[] Flucht ins gute Gewissen des morgigen Tages'. (398) Thus Kirill's predicament of having to choose between his love for Tamila and his obligation towards Laura, of having to make a choice between change and status quo, becomes a crucial test of character, for in a situation where everybody else would have jumped at the opportunity offered, Kirill hesitates:

> Dieser unvergeßliche Augenblick hätte jedem anderen die glück-lichste Gelegenheit geboten – und jeder andere hätte sie auch genützt –, einen unerträglichen Zustand gegen einen paradiesi-schen einzutauschen . . . Mich aber entsetzte mitten im Glück . . . , daß noch vor Stunden dasselbe Glück aus einer andern Herzens-wunde geschossen . . . (414–15)

Having prevaricated for a while, he eventually arrives at the cru-cial conclusion that 'mit Laura verbindet mich *die Treue zu mir selbst* – welche der Grund aller Treue ist! – und von Tamila trennt mich die Furcht vor allem, was *Veränderung* nach sich zieht, oder gar Bekehrung verursachen könnte [*my italics*]' (406–7),[37] and that even the slightest neglect of duty would open the flood gates and set in motion a chain reaction:

> Nur so viel weiß man, daß ein winziger Akt des Verrats, ein kleines Aufatmen über gestrichene Pflichten . . . genügen, um den nur leicht gleitenden Vorhang des unbekannten Schauspiels aufgehen zu machen, in welchem Schauspiel dann bald . . . geredet wird als von wieder einem Vorhang, der auch noch sich würde heben, und so fort; denn mit dem Verrat ist's wie mit dem Trinken . . . (416)

In other words, decisions made on the spur of the moment must never be allowed to obviate years spent in building up a relation-ship, and time must not be allowed to take its toll:

> der Vorrang in der Zeit ist ein gewichtiger Vorrang. Die Kürze des Menschenlebens fordert, daß zwei Jahre, in aufrichtiger Wer-bung hingebracht, nicht mit dem Maß der Tagediebe gemessen werden . . . Sie fordert, daß eine Stunde nicht umstürzen darf, woran so viele ihrer Schwestern gebaut haben. (418)

Ultimately therefore, Kirill's intense hatred of all things new ('leidenschaftlich[er] Haß gegen das Neue' (433)) prevails, mirrored in the stark contrast of Tamila's world of constant change, and that of her aristocratic lover devoted to the permanency of the status quo:

> wir alle wollen ja gerade, was du Merkwürdiger fürchtest: durch Vergessen, durch Verlassen, durch Verrat . . . neu werden, böse, wenn das Alte gut, gut, wenn das Alte böse gewesen ist. Wie anders auch sollte das große Rad dieses Lebens vorwärts gehen. (425)[38]

The preceding analysis thus confirms that *Eine sagenhafte Figur* is essentially a novel of ideas.[39] None the less, historical events and timeless problems are inextricably linked in this work, the Great War being the 'äußere Erscheinungsform geistiger Auseinandersetzungen einer gährenden Zeit'.[40] Kirill Ostrog, Gütersloh's protagonist, is a representative of this period: the Habsburg Empire during the twilight of its existence. Presented as an anachronistic figure, a late-comer[41] on the threshold of a new era, living in both past and future without belonging to either,[42] he is an anti-hero *par excellence*,[43] opposed to change of any kind, living in accordance with his own high moral standards: 'nicht Anwalt irgendeiner Ordnung, sondern einfach ein Mensch von hervorragender Sittlichkeit.'[44]

Despite a certain lack of historical detail, the impression is difficult to avoid, though, that *Eine sagenhafte Figur* is also an allegorical novel in disguise,[45] suspended at a point of intellectual upheaval ('Punkt ideengeschichtlicher Umwälzungen'),[46] an 'analogy between individual strife and collective combat'.[47] Kirill's personality traits, especially his decadence, mirror similar features prevalent in the Austro-Hungarian Empire during the final period of its existence; his total rejection of change is comparable with the resistance to changes on a much larger scale within the socio-political structure of the Habsburg Empire, a *Todestanz* lasting from the *fin de siècle* to the outbreak of the First World War, as Hansjörg Graf perceptively argued:

> Gütersloh hat den endgültigen Zerfall eines Reiches, in dem 'die Sonne nie untergegangen ist', erlebt; dieser Untergang und die mit ihm definitiv versäumten Möglichkeiten sind für Gütersloh

der Grundstoff, aus dem er seine allegorischen Phantasien und Exkurse entwickelt, insbesondere im Interludium von *Sonne und Mond*. In diesem Interludium, das wir vielleicht als ein imaginäres Gespräch des Autors mit der jungen Republik Österreich deuten dürfen, betritt Gütersloh die vulkanische Landschaft der 'politischen Theologie'. Die konkrete Ausgangsposition für alle Ausflüge dieser Art bleibt 1914.[48]

Writing *Eine sagenhafte Figur* in the late 1920s, Gütersloh undoubtedly drew on personal memories of the pre-First World War era; similarly, the concept of the ninth chapter in *Sonne und Mond* – a 'historischer Roman aus der Gegenwart' – evolved during the early 1940s, when the author was officially banned from writing,[49] and reflects his experience of the inter-war period.

In *Sonne und Mond* Gütersloh compares the Austria of the Habsburg days – the dilapidated residence symbolizes 'Alt-Österreich'[50] – and that of the First Republic, alluding to historical events in the crypto-totalitarian *Ständestaat* under Dollfuß after 1934, and, in passing, to the period after the *Anschluß* in 1938, when Austria became part of a fully fledged fascist dictatorship.[51] Consequently, the assumption does not seem too far-fetched – echoing Graf's interpretation of the 'Interludium' in *Sonne und Mond*[52] – that in *Eine sagenhafte Figur* Gütersloh was having a similar kind of imaginary dialogue with the old Austria before 1914, as in *Sonne und Mond* with the new Austria after 1918–19, even if the dialogue in the earlier novel ends with a gesture of resigned heroism and regret.[53]

Notes

1. Albert Paris Gütersloh was the assumed pen-name of Albert Conrad Kiehtreiber.
2. For a brief biographical overview of Gütersloh's life see Ludwig Fischer, 'Albert Paris Gütersloh', in Donald G. Daviau (ed.), *Major Figures of Modern Austrian Literature* (Riverside, CA, 1988), pp. 209–10.
3. An official post-war copy (9 September 1945) of the 1938 letter (P.Z. 54–1938) by the then director of the Academy of Applied Arts, Professor Robert Obsieger, states:

Die Enthebung des Professors Gütersloh erfolgte auf Grund eines Antrages der NSDAP. Seine Tätigkeit als kommunistischer Schriftsteller [sic], die schlechte pädagogische Führung und schlechte künstlerische Leistung seiner Klasse, die vorwiegend als Kunstentartung bezeichnet wird, schliessen eine Weiterverwendung an der Kunstgewerbeschule aus.

4 Issued by the 'Landesleiter der Reichskammer der bildenden Künste beim Landeskulturverwalter Gau Wien' on 13 February 1941.

5 Cf. Herbert Eisenreich, 'Gütersloh, Albert Paris', in *Handbuch der deutschen Gegenwartsliteratur* (Munich, 1965), pp. 225–6.

6 These two novels, plus the programmatic essay *Die Rede über Franz Blei oder Der Schriftsteller in der Katholizität* (1922), were published with Hegner of Hellerau near Dresden.

7 Cf. Fischer, 'Gütersloh', pp. 210–11; Edwin Hartl thought of APG as an 'eminent unbekannte[] Berühmtheit' (in 'Gütersloh – den gibt es wirklich', *Wort in der Zeit*, No.3 (1963), 36).

8 *Kain und Abel. Eine Legende* (1924), and *Der Maler Alexander Gartenberg* (1928).

9 Cf. letter of 14 June 1995 by Dr Irmgard Hutter (Vienna), Gütersloh's 'Nachlaßverwalterin', who transcribed most of the writer's manuscripts, and to whom I am indebted for this, and numerous other, items of information:

In den 30er Jahren war die ökonomische und politische Situation in Österreich so miserabel, daß an Publikation der SF nicht zu denken war. Rudolf Haybach, der bis zu Doderers 'Fall Gütersloh' 1930 engagiert blieb, hatte kein Geld mehr; andere Versuche, einen Verleger zu finden, schlugen fehl. Auch Bleis Vermittlungsversuche nützten nichts. Auf dem winzigen österreichischen Markt konnte niemand wagen, ein unverkäufliches Buch zu verlegen, und der größere deutsche war bald verschlossen ... Die Zeitumstände waren so ungünstig, daß APG ca. ab 1933/34 sich nicht mehr bemüht haben dürfte, den Roman unterzubringen.

10 The earliest mention of *Eine sagenhafte Figur* dates from 19 April 1927 in Gütersloh's notebook of 1927–8 ('Notizbuch 1927–28'/Ser.n.33.606); further date references occur in 'Notizbuch I' (Ser.n.33.016/6 April– 25 September 1928); 'Notizbuch II' (Ser.n.33.017/13 March 1929); and 'Notizbuch III' (Ser.n.33.018/3 June–23 July 1930); these manuscripts are part of the Gütersloh-'Nachlaß' at the Österreichische National-bibliothek (Vienna). The bulk of the manuscript seems to have been written in Cagnes-sur-mer on the French Riviera, the remainder in Vienna. The second version of the manuscript ('Reinschrift'/Vienna 1930–1) belongs to Angela Pauser (Rudolf Haybach's former girl-friend); a typewritten manuscript (third version), containing extensive

handwritten alterations by APG (also at the ÖNB), seems to have been produced prior to the book publication with Luckmann in 1946; the same applies to the composition of the afterword ('Nachwort in Usum Delphini'), which Gütersloh appended to the novel after the war.

[11] Unfortunately, the Munich-based Piper Verlag, which reissued a number of Gütersloh's works in paperback (Serie Piper) since the 1980s, recently cancelled arrangements for future – additional – publications; for bibliographical details see Hans F. Prokop, 'Albert Paris Gütersloh: Bibliographie', *Literatur und Kritik*, 68 (1972), 483–92.

[12] Michael Bielefeld, 'Albert Paris Gütersloh', in Heinz Ludwig Arnold (ed.), *Kritisches Lexikon zur deutschsprachigen Gegenwartsliteratur*, vol. 3 (Munich, 1985), 1–12 and A–F, refers to the 'Thema der Spannung von Wahrheit und Lüge' in Gütersloh's work (4).

[13] Cf. Felix Thurner, *Albert Paris Gütersloh. Studien zu seinem Romanwerk* (Bern, 1970) (= ch.IV, 87–109), here p. 92; other commentators have adopted a more critical view of Gütersloh's extensive use of dialogic exchanges in *Eine sagenhafte Figur*; cf. e.g. Adelbert Muhr's comment: 'von einer Handlung [ist] kaum etwas zu spüren, alles überwuchert des Autors platonisches Philosophieren' (in 'Buchbesprechungen – A. P. Gütersloh: "Eine Sagenhafte Figur"', *Wort und Tat*, No. 5 (1947), 130).

[14] Gütersloh's 'Nachwort' to *Eine sagenhafte Figur*, added after World War II, must be considered an artistic failure (cf. Thurner, op. cit., p. 88).

[15] Thurner, op. cit., p. 92.

[16] Bielefeld, op. cit., p. 2.

[17] Ibid., p. 3.

[18] Ibid., p. 7.

[19] Cf. Otto Basil, 'Panorama vom Untergang Kakaniens', *Wort in der Zeit*, No. 7 (1961), 23–35.

[20] Bielefeld, op. cit., 3.

[21] Thurner, op. cit., p. 96.

[22] The text proper runs to 443 pages; the remainder is devoted to the afterword, which Gütersloh appended after the war.

[23] Thurner, op. cit., p. 88.

[24] Fischer, op. cit., p. 223.

[25] The text used here is that of the first edition: *Eine sagenhafte Figur. Ein platonischer Roman mit einem Nachwort in Usum Delphini* (Vienna, 1946); page references following citations in brackets refer to this edition (here p. 150); the novel was reissued in 1985 (= Serie Piper 372).

[26] Cf. Heribert Hutter's introduction 'Apokalyptisches Reden "Der Fall Gütersloh"' to Jeremy Adler (ed.), *Allegorie und Eros. Texte von und mit Albert Paris Gütersloh* (München/Zürich, 1986), p. 13: 'Vor diesem Hintergrund gewinnen die Figuren Güterslohs . . . gleichnishafte

Bedeutung für die Schwierigkeit, wenn nicht Unmöglichkeit, . . . das
für richtig Erkannte auch auf geradem Wege zu erreichen.'

27 While getting ready for his physical before the draft board, Kirill
muses about the impending war and the nature of change: 'Es ver-
halte sich mit dem Recht zu einem Kriege, wie immer: wir haben
nach innen, wie nach außen nur einen einzigen, wirklichen Feind: die
Veränderung [*my italics*].' (p. 325).

28 Cf. Hansjörg Graf, 'Proteus der alten Welt. Über Albert Paris Güter-
sloh', *Der Monat*, No. 203 (1965), 75; Frank Trommler (in *Roman und
Wirklichkeit. Eine Ortsbestimmung am Beispiel von Musil, Broch, Roth,
Doderer und Gütersloh* (Stuttgart, 1966), p. 160), considers 'heftige
Beichten [und] heftige Dialoge, die von Gütersloh bevorzugte Aus-
sageform'.

29 Thurner, op. cit., p. 106, noted that 'Güterslohs Figurenwelt fast
zwangsläufig paarig konzipiert [ist]'.

30 According to Thurner, op. cit., p. 95, Gütersloh was familiar with the
work of the Viennese philosopher Otto Weininger (1880–1903), and in
particular his famous study *Geschlecht und Charakter* (1903), espousing
a theory of the conflict of the sexes.

31 Cf. Muhr, op. cit., p. 130, who noted that Kirill's 'Zwitterleben' is neither that of a monk or a roué ('weder Mönch noch Wüstling').

32 At a much earlier stage Bettina prophetically proclaimed that for
Kirill the war was nothing but a golden opportunity ('Gelegenheit'
(198)) to uphold the status quo of his existing life-style.

33 'Mein Wesen ist keine Rolle, die ich Ihretwegen erfunden habe', Kirill
informs his fellow volunteer. (317)

34 Later, having been himself rejected by the draft board, Kirill admits to
his earlier mendacious conduct: 'Da . . ., von einer schönen Lüge aus-
gefüllt, . . . wanderte er [the young volunteer/JT] ins Falsche. Ein
wertvolles Wesen zerstreute sich ins Leere. Mit jedem Schritt ging er
dem Abgrund zu, häufte er, ein schlecht beratner Schüler, Schuld auf
das Haupt des Meisters.' (334)

35 Since coming of age, Kirill – having officially gained access to a personal fortune – is one of the wealthiest men in the country.

36 According to the vagabond 'die meisten Menschen spielen eine Rolle
und die wenigsten sind Zuschauer'. (p. 349)

37 Graf, op. cit., p. 77, considers this to be a 'Schlüsselsatz zum Verständ-
nis eines Dichters, dem dialogisches Leben primär Selbstgespräch ist'.

38 A point admitted by Kirill himself at an earlier stage of the novel
while talking to the young army volunteer: 'Der Gute möchte gern
den Bösen ablösen, denn er ist ja gut. Der Böse möchte gern das
höhere Sein des Guten annehmen, denn er ist ja nicht wirklich böse.
Sie möchten einander so gern auf der Mitte des Schaukelbrettes
umarmen. . . . Aber: wenn dies geschähe, stünde das Brett still. Die

Welt ginge nicht mehr vorwärts. Das letzte Reich bräche nie an.'
(318–19)

[39] Cf. Fischer, op..cit., p. 222.

[40] Thurner, op. cit., p. 97.

[41] Ibid., p. 100.

[42] Ibid., p. 95; cf. also Walter Höllerer, 'Albert Paris Gütersloh', *Welt-Stimmen*, 2 No. 7 (1953), 326, who maintains that Kirill is 'mit der Vergangenheit verfilzt und ins Zukünftige verlangend, den Revolutionären ein Konservativer und den Konservativen ein Revolutionär . . .'

[43] Cf. Graf's characterization of Kirill as an 'Antiheld *par excellence* (op. cit., p. 76); Thurner's portrayal of Kirill as a 'fast ein positiver Held' (op. cit., p. 93) is wide of the mark though.

[44] Thurner, op. cit., p. 99.

[45] Cf. the entry on 'allegory' in Gero von Wilpert's *Sachwörterbuch der Literatur*, 7th edn (Stuttgart, 1989), 18–19.

[46] Thurner, op. cit., p. 96.

[47] Cf. Fischer: 'Subconscious feelings of failure, anger and hostility surface as an armed struggle on the conscious level' (op. cit., pp. 222–3).

[48] Graf, op. cit., p. 77.

[49] Cf. the 'Interludium oder IX. Kapitel' in *Sonne und Mond. Ein historischer Roman aus der Gegenwart* (Munich, 1984); pp. 551–641, esp. pp. 575–641.

[50] Cf. Otto F. Beer, 'Albert Paris Gütersloh. "Die letzte große Barockfigur Österreichs"', *Die Zeit*, No. 22 (25 May 1973), 22.

[51] Cf. Gütersloh's unpublished work 'Zwischenstufen' (1938ff.), pp. 199–201 (typewritten MS).

[52] Cf. Hansjörg Graf, 'Der Schlüssel zum Schloß. Notizen zu A. P. Gütersloh "Sonne und Mond"', in *Albert Paris Gütersloh. Zum 75. Geburtstag* (Munich, 1962), 40–5, esp. pp. 41–2.

[53] Thurner, op. cit., p. 99.